BABA AMTE

BABA AMTE
A Biography

ANITA KAINTHLA

Viva Books

New Delhi | Mumbai | Chennai | Kolkata | Bengaluru | Hyderabad | Kochi | Guwahati

Publisher's note

Every possible effort has been made to ensure that the information contained in this book is accurate at the time of going to press, and the publisher and author cannot accept responsibility for any errors or omissions, however caused. No responsibility for loss or damage occasioned to any person acting, or refraining from action, as a result of the material in this publication can be accepted by the editor, the publisher or the author.

Every effort has been made to trace the owners of copyright material used in this book. The author and the publisher will be grateful for any omission brought to their notice for acknowledgement in the future editions of the book.

First Published 2005
Reprinted 2006, 2012, 2019, 2025

Viva Books Private Limited

- 4737/23, Ansari Road, Daryaganj, New Delhi 110 002
  Tel. 42242200, 23258325, 23283121, Email: vivadelhi@vivagroupindia.in
- 76, Service Industries, Shirvane, Sector 1, Nerul, Navi Mumbai 400 706
  Tel. 27721273, 27721274, Email: vivamumbai@vivagroupindia.in
- Jamals Fazal Chambers, 26 Greams Road, Chennai 600 006
  Tel. 28294241, 28290304, Email: vivachennai@vivagroupindia.in
- B-103, Jindal Towers, 21/1A/3 Darga Road, Kolkata 700 017
  Tel. 22816713, Email: vivakolkata@vivagroupindia.in
- 7, GF, Sovereign Park Aptts., 56-58, K. R. Road, Basavanagudi, Bengaluru 560 004
  Tel. 26607409, Email: vivabangalore@vivagroupindia.in
- 101-102, Moghal Marc Apartments, 3-4-637 to 641, Narayanguda, Hyderabad 500 029
  Tel. 27564481, Email: vivahyderabad@vivagroupindia.in
- First Floor, Beevi Towers, SRM Road, Kaloor, Kochi 682 018
  Tel. 0484-2403055, 2403056, Email: vivakochi@vivagroupindia.in
- 232, GNB Road, Beside UCO Bank, Silpukhuri, Guwahati 781 003
  Tel. 0361-2666386, Email: vivaguwahati@vivagroupindia.in

www.vivagroupindia.com

ISBN: 978-81-309-0099-5

Published by Viva Books Private Limited, 4737/23 Ansari Road, Daryaganj, New Delhi 110 002.

Printed and bound in India by Replika Press Pvt. Ltd.

Dedication

To my family, my support system

Contents

Foreword

When I first met Baba Amte in early 1990s, he made a vivid impression on me. In southern India, on what was previously barren earth he has brought into existence a thriving community surrounded by trees, a rose garden and a vegetable garden. It is provided with a small hospital, an old people's home, schools and workshops. This alone is a great achievement, but what makes the place remarkable is that it was built entirely by handicapped people. In creating Anandwan he provided a practical opportunity for people even with crucial disadvantages to show that they could regain diginity and come to be recognized as productive members of society.

Baba Amte is an extraordinary person. After a long, vigorous life, during which he has suffered great physical hardship, because of damage to his spine, he can only stand straight or lie down. Yet he remains so full of energy and does things I could not think of doing myself, despite being fit. As I sat on his bed holding his hand, and he lay talking to me, I could not help feeling that here was someone who was truly compassionate. I told him that whereas my compassion is just so much talk, his shone through in everything he did. Then Baba Amte told me how he made the decision to dedicate his life to helping others. One day, he met a leper with worms in the place where his eyes had been. That was all it took.

I felt that people of Baba Amte's calibre are so rare in our world and yet provide such an inspiration to us all that it is important that their stories should be told. Therefore, I congratulate the author of this biography, Anita Kainthla, for presenting an accessible and straightforward account of a man who has consistently put others before himself; a living example of true compassion in action.

November 16, 2004

(HIS HOLINESS THE DALAI LAMA)

Introduction

The manner in which Murlidhar Devidas Amte stumbled upon the maggot-infested leper, Tulsiram, similarly I happened to stumble upon Amte's story. In December 2002, there appeared a slice of the life of Baba Amte by Malavika Sanghavi in the Sunday Magazine of *The Times of India.* It was the first time that I ever reread a piece of news; I doubted its veracity. But soon shame replaced disbelief – there were many people I'd met, known, heard of and read of, but Baba Amte's name merely hovered precariously in the periphery of such a list of people when it should have topped the list. The manner in which Amte became restless after his encounter with Tulsiram, I thirsted for the entire, almost unbelievable story of Baba Amte.

After visiting '*The Man*' himself several times in his 'Garden of Joy' – Anandwan – I was filled with wonder and amazement as the story of this unusual man who had lived an unusual life doing unusual work, was unfurled. The urge to write of such a life as Amte's could not have been far.

I went from surprise to shock on discovering that Baba Amte's life had always only been the subject of news items, with hardly anyone ever knowing the whole truth of his tremendously invigorating tale. He has even ceased to be the subject of a news on item for a couple of years now. On 26th December 2004 Murlidhar Devidas Amte turned 90 – no word, no news, no line in any of our prestigious dailies, weeklies, etc., which eulogize not only births and deaths but even engagements and accidents of cine and sports stars!

These are the icons that we are forcing upon the impressionable urban youth. And in addition to our own 'stars', the Dianas, Beckhams and Lopezes are doing the rounds of the lives of our young urban Indians. While it is we who have begun the disintegration of culture, we hypocritically bemoan it and blame it on the younger lot. When the likes of Murlidhar Devidas Amte are still around, we need only to tell their stories more clearly and loudly in order for the right kind of motivation and inspiration to reach our young urbanites. Through this biography I have attempted to bring one of the most inspirational stories of our lifetimes from the obscurity of the interiors of Maharashtra, in an attempt to brighten the lives of the urban youth who are straying into dark alleys.

CHAPTER 1

Vis-à-vis the Man

Born on 26th December 1914, to Sh. Devidas and Smt. Laxmibai Amte of Hinganghat in Warora district of Maharashtra, Baba Amte was initially christened Murlidhar Devidas Amte. His family on both sides comprised tradition- bound landed gentry. His father worked as a middle-level government officer during British rule. Murlidhar was amongst the affluent and lucky few of those days and hence received a wholesome education. He acquired a law degree from the law college at Nagpur and became a practising lawyer.

His over-sensitive temperament began picking up the pangs of the caste-ridden and impoverished society as early as adolescence. But his many attempts to reach out to his discarded and destitute fellowmen met with stiff resistance from both his father as well as society in general. Armed with his mother's legacy of a rebellious nature and the strong influences of Gandhi, Tagore and Vinoba Bhave, Murlidhar fought all resistance and even forsook the comforts of life. He became an ascetic.

Taking a vow of celibacy, he left home. But destiny had yet other designs for him. While attending the wedding of a relative, he crossed paths with a pretty, petite and an intensely humane girl, Indu. He made up his mind in a single encounter with her. He approached her parents and asked for her hand in marriage. Once again fingers, eyebrows and voices were all raised against him. He suffered another bout of resistance. His matted locks, saintly attire and vow of celibacy all stood between him and Indu. But marry her he would, so he broke his vow and brought home his bride.

Thereafter, Murlidhar took up life from where he had left. This time round, he found support in his better half. This egged him on. He began organizing the downtrodden into unions and fought for their rights. He even began to live and work like them in order to have a feel of their plight.

One day he literally stumbled upon a man so terribly afflicted with leprosy that what little remained of his body barely suggested he was once human. At first Murli fled in fear but later returned on realizing that the only way to mitigate the monster of fear was to replace it with love. In the process, Murli found his calling. From thereon he devoted himself to the service of those affected with the least communicable of all communicable diseases – leprosy.

In all this Indu was the only one who stood steadfast behind the man she had married. As for his father and society in general, the chasm between them and him deepened and widened day by day. It was an unpardonable crime by their standards for a high-caste and affluent Hindu young man to take even a casual interest in the lowly, let alone fight for and serve them. And when the chasm so deepened that neither party could see the other's side, Murli decided it was time to move on. With two infants, a young wife, a lame cow, four stray dogs, six lepers and Rs. 14 in his pocket, he left home and moved house to a leaf-thatched shelter in the midst of 50 acres of rocky, arid land, 5km short of Warora. Amte, who now had come to be known as 'Baba', named that place Anandwan.

Anandwan, or the 'Garden of Bliss', was ironically described by Baba as 'an outcaste land for an outcaste man' because the barren acres there were beset with huge boulders, deep-rooted bushes and trees. This land of 50 acres given to Baba by the Madhya Pradesh government was part of a disused quarry. Here, he set up a small institution called the Maharogi Sewa Samiti (MSS), with the aid of sheer will and faith in hard labour and also the support of his wife and a few well-wishers. This place became home to them along with cured and convalescing leprosy patients, which today are a strong 5000 in number.

Before setting out to meet *the Man* himself, I had read only this broad outline of Baba Amte's life story. Just a little homework on his beginnings and bearings was enough to meet my requirements. I felt it was not right to prejudice my impressions with second-hand stories. I thought it would be better to get some first-hand facts in order to recreate the sublimity of his life with words. Hence, I set out with only a few fragments from an unparalleled saga of sacrifice and service.

My journey to Anandwan was motivated by these sketchy details that I had from a delightful picture. Therefore, my eagerness to visit the place, meet the man and complete the picture was understandable.

From Delhi to Nagpur, the train journey of twenty-two hours seemed to last till eternity. At Nagpur I unboarded the train with a head occupied with echoes of varied hues assimilated during the journey and a pair of unsteady legs due to sitting for so long. But Anandwan could be reached only after another three hours of drive from Nagpur. I hired a rickety taxi, playing Hindi film music in just a little less than full volume, further aggravating my woes. On the road to Warora, there was little that hit the eye. But beyond a hundred kilometres from Nagpur, the barren brown and jaded green of the familiar windswept landscape suddenly turned darker and greener. Obviously people had been at work and nature, in turn, had been freely letting them into her secrets. Here, I was told, lived the communes of Anandwan. Before long, thanks to the overspeeding taxi, I was at Anandwan. My anxiety to be inside the place won an emphatic victory over my tiredness.

We entered Anandwan, I moved closer to the edge of the seat and to the window and peered out. A reasonably wide and well-metalled road ran before us as far as the eye could see. As we rolled on over the road, on either side we saw various structures – housing quarters, an array of shops, a flourishing nursery of ornamental plants, a plastic recycling unit, a cowshed with dozens of milch cattle, etc. Just a little ahead of the cowshed, the road bifurcated and the taxi was stopped by a middle-aged man. It was Avinash Sathate, the secretary and first inmate of Anandwan I met.

After an exchange of pleasantries and introductions, I was happy to know that my arrival had been expected. Avinash ushered me into a wall-less, roofed extension of a cluster of buildings. Seating myself on a narrow wooden sofa, I looked around. In addition to a couple of chairs and a huge settee, there was another sofa of the kind I sat in, covered with a duree (mat) and sprinkled generously with cushions and bolsters. In the centre was a large granite table top resting on a huge boulder on which lay several newspapers and magazines. Avinash ordered tea. Even as I took the first sip of the thick sweet syrupy tea, there was a pleasant commotion outside. The chirping suggested that the birds were back home to roost. 'It's the parrots. Come and look outside,' Avinash said. Parrots they were, but it was their number that was astounding. On almost every branch of every tree there were as many parrots as there were leaves. It seemed that the trees were a parrot green in shade which had sprung to life, sprouted beaks and were chirping to their hearts' content. Such was the commotion that we had to raise our voices considerably in order to hear each other.

'These are friends of Anandwan,' said Avinash, the joy and pride all too evident in his smile. As suddenly as the commotion had started, it died down too – the birds had settled in for a night-long slumber.

I put down my empty tea cup. A young man with a pronounced limp as well as a smile sauntered in and told me that my room was ready. This young man was a cured leprosy patient. Avinash pulled up the man's pyjamas and showed me his footless leg.

I was shown into my room by the duo. The modest room was spotless. Three cots covered with mosquito nets and clean sheets, a small table and a cupboard. The bare essentials seemed more than sufficient for my needs. The spacious bathroom had a geyser, but more importantly, a 24-hour water supply!

A hot bath and a set of fresh clothes drove away the exhaustion of the long journey to a large extent. Sprawling on the bed, I began leafing through the brochures that Avinash had given me, trying to acquaint myself with Anandwan and its dwellers. There was a knock on the door. The smiling lame boy standing outside informed me that dinner was ready. It would be served in a refectory and I was required to follow him there. Strapping on my sandals, I followed my guide. The refectory was about 60-70 metres from the room. Before entering I took off my sandals and washed my hands, keeping with the tradition of the place but was hardly prepared for what met my eyes.

The figure of the person who stood with his back facing the entrance was very familiar. Dressed in a pair of longish white shorts and a vest, back supported by a brace and a head with an unruly crop of silver hair – this was *the Man* himself! Murlidhar Devidas Amte, now addressed fondly as Baba Amte, stood facing, thankfully, away from me. I had just a few minutes to prepare myself for the first encounter. As I walked into the largish refectory set with a number of dining chairs and tables, I noticed that Baba was just finishing his dinner. His attendant stood besides him helping him to wind up. Indu, now addressed as Sadhana Tai, was sitting a couple of seats away from Baba and she too was busy with her dinner. Another thing I noticed was that Baba was standing and eating. 'Odd', I thought. Later on inquiry, however, I learned that he was afflicted with a degenerative spine disease and had six of his vertebrae surgically removed. He could either lie flat on his back or just stand. For the last 22 years, from 1980 to 2002, he had not been able to sit! Walking with head lowered, I chose an empty table and sat down and then urged myself to be bold enough to steal glances at the man, standing a few paces away from me. 'Maybe I will get to meet him tomorrow,' I thought to myself.

No sooner had I settled in my seat than a smiling young girl laid a steel plate and several bowls in front of me. Just behind her stood another girl with a large bowl of dal (lentil soup), ready to ladle it into my plate. Then one after another, vegetables, salads, pickles, chappatis, rice and curds were all served to me. Eyes lowered, I began to eat. Even as I raised a morsel midway to my mouth, I saw Baba leave the table. But he was not heading out, instead he began walking in my direction. I dropped the morsel back into the plate and stood up. Upon reaching me Baba folded his hands and with a hearty smile looked straight into my eyes.

'*Namaskar*', I said.

He nodded and looked into my plate.

'I hope you like the food,' he said. His speech was very slurred. 89 years, a horde of ailments and the drugs he had to take for them were all responsible for his speech.

'Oh yes. It's perfect,' I replied.

'I hope it's not too spicy for you?' the concern in his voice was genuine.

'Its just fine,' I assured him.

Satisfied, he folded his hands and turned to leave supported by his attendant. The attendant flashed a smile at me. I was astonished that smiles were so common here. As though the people here, the last, the least and the lowest, were always happy. They indeed were, I later found out.

In a few seconds Baba was out of the door and the refectory. I sat down to resume eating and to reorganize my thoughts that had been thrown into a bit of a frenzy due to the unexpected encounter. One of the many girls who had served me, came up to me with a smile that I had grown to expect in such a short time.

'You're lucky to have met Baba on the first day,' she said before bidding me a good night. It was a happy thought to sleep with on my first day at Anandwan.

CHAPTER 2

Women behind the Scenes

GROWING UP WITH AAI (MOTHER)

Baba was born at the beginning of the First World War, during which the first seeds of so much of today's suffering were sown. His mother Laxmibai was travelling by train when she experienced the pangs of labour. Unboarding the train midway, at Hinganghat, she delivered the baby, later named Murlidhar.

He found himself born into a family where the father's conservative notions about social class and status were strictly enforced. Murlidhar received formal education. He attended Rama Krishna Mission School in Warora, Maharashtra. The children of the family were barred from bonding and breaking bread with the servants of the house and others of the lower castes. Neither deviation from these norms nor any expression of difference of opinion and rebellion in thought or action was tolerated. He remembers that when he travelled as a child in a bullock cart, a servant used to run ahead and announce that someone of repute was approaching.

Laxmibai was the only one who dared to question such rigidities of traditions in the Amte household. 'She was always up in arms against Bapuji's (father's) views on various issues,' recalled Baba. He added, 'the germs of rebellion would have entered my blood through her.' From early childhood, the boy was a puzzle to his father, a stern and distant man and a dutiful government official, for Murlidhar was consistently and congenitally irreverent. As a schoolboy in a red blazer, he was often seen with a can of worms and a fishing rod, whistling off on his way to catch fish. And a good Brahmin was not supposed to take life. At 14 he slipped away from home to learn hunting from the Madia Gonds, the tribals deep in the Gadchiroli forests.

Unfortunately, even when Murlidhar was very young, as a result of some domestic conflict, which much exceeded her endurance limit, Laxmibai fell prey to acute psychosis. Her mental illness, however, never mitigated the son's admiration for the mother. 'My mother was really a courageous woman and was my ideal. I did not carry much respect for Bapuji [father],' says Baba. His voice becomes distant as his mind flies back to his beloved mother, an old-fashioned, generous mad woman. 'She was an uneducated artist and did go mad. But she helped me keep myself sane in an insane world,' he added. In an article 'My Mother's Madness', written in Marathi by Baba, his affection for his mother is amply evident:

> While I was taking refuge in poetry, wrestling, hunting, mother was in hospital.
>
> Amongst the mad women there were a few who were young and pretty. Some doctors and other members of the hospital staff would take advantage of their mental state and sexually exploit them. Many of them had actually taken up jobs in order to exploit these women. Since the women were mad, they could neither comprehend nor report the ill-deeds of these people to the authorities. But mother kept an eye on the goings on in the hospital. When senior officials came for an inspection of the place, she reported to these people along with some evidence that she had collected. Due to her efforts a young doctor and some other people were suspended.
>
> Once the daughter-in-law of a session's judge was admitted to the hospital. Having lost her husband at a young age, she could not tolerate her misfortune and became mad. Mother first slowly won her confidence through affection and then began looking after her. She would not listen to anyone but mother. Mother also could not live without her. In one year the two became very close and then mother was discharged from the hospital. When I went to pick her up, she was reluctant to leave the young woman and come away with me. She said that she was finding it difficult to leave someone who was so entirely dependant on her. The woman was sleeping on the floor and mother was affectionately running her fingers through her hair.

In the same hospital mother had made another good friend, an Anglo-Indian nurse named Mrs. Lipton. Mother was very pleased with the dedication of Mrs. Lipton to her patients. My mother had ordered me to bring sweets for Mrs. Lipton whenever I visited her. When mother came home, she invited Mrs. Lipton to dinner and presented her with a watch. Mrs. Lipton said that as long as her left hand was attached to her body she would remember mother. Later when Mrs. Lipton went to England, she wrote letters to mother, which I would read out to her.

Mother was only admitted once to the mental hospital, but she developed a strong bond with all the inmates there. Though for father she was still mad, for others she was kind and affectionate.

There was a Brahmin's daughter, who was very beautiful but mad. When she would feed her child, she would roam around nude. She would bathe in the open and people would stare at her from far as she was very beautiful. However no one would dare come near her as a wrestler by the name of Gulab Kadir would always be there to guard her. One day mother invited this wrestler home and fed him. Then she called me and said, 'This man saw only how a mother fed her child, he did not see her nudity. You should be like him, like Lord Bajrang Bali.'

When the medicines were proving ineffective in improving mother's condition, father called a man who was adept in black magic. But mother lashed out at him as soon as she saw him, 'You think you will cure my madness? Who are you? God is the one who does everything. He has made me mad, only he can cure me. You go away from here.' Mother did not believe in superstitions and rituals. She was always unafraid to voice her anger.

As before, mother began abusing father. She would scream and sing loudly in the night, so that father could not sleep peacefully. But father never lost his temper. He was very patient with mother. For forty years he stayed with a mad woman. We never saw them living separately.

Endowed with the traits of curiosity and questioning, of rebellion against rigid, meaningless norms, Baba appeared distinct from the rest of the brood. He was not the one to blindly follow his father's unwritten code of conduct that the rest of the siblings had embraced. 'Why should the family lands have to be tilled by others, who live in poverty while we enjoy the fruits of their hard, backbreaking toil?' he asked.

'Why am I not allowed to share food with them?' 'Who is to be blamed for this disparity? Why was it made?' he further questioned. 'To me the ideas and conduct of my father and his class seemed not merely rigid but downright petrified,' he recalled later.

When he found no satisfactory answers to these queries, he began to mix around with all classes and creeds of children. He shared food, played and even visited their homes. When he showed no signs of relenting, his father nicknamed him 'Dalubai' (miller). And later he rechristened him 'Don Quxiote', when he helped his mother with her backbreaking chores.

But Baba was not recalcitrant without reason. He was born with a humane heart that was pained by disparities between humans on the basis of caste and creed. The partially demented and generous Laxmibai hugged her dear son, eleven at that time, and lovingly kissed him on the forehead for an act of charity.

> I was a boy when my mad mother gave me a whole load of coins for celebrating Diwali as I wanted to. I was rushing to the market to buy sweets when I saw a blind beggar in the hot sun saying, '*andhalaya paisa dey*' (give a penny to the blind man).
>
> I put all the coins in his tin box and he pleaded not to put stones into the box. After depositing the coins, I stood aside as the beggar felt the coins and started counting them with an occasional blessing.
>
> I went home with some fear and told everything to my mother. She hugged and kissed me. That imprint of the kiss I still carry on my forehead.

When Baba was in high school, his father retired from government service and moved house to Dharampeth – a posh area of a larger town Nagpur. There he joined the Morris and Hislop College. After gaining a B.A. degree from college, he studied at the government law school, graduating with a law degree in 1936. He would have preferred to have studied medicine but yielded to his father's wishes and entered the legal profession.

Apart from his courageous mother, there were others who inspired him. There were the revolutionaries, principally Mahatma Gandhi. 'I would run away from home leaving a note in the holy books to become a revolutionary,' he says. Tagore, who was awarded the Nobel Prize for literature in 1913, caught his fancy at the age of eleven with *Geetanjali*. He learnt Bengali in order to read the book. Later he even visited Tagore at Shantiniketan, a microcosm of Tagore's ideal world, and stayed with him for a while. Closer home was Sewagram, where a new paradigm of development was being forged by Mahatma Gandhi, as an integral part of the struggle against British colonial rule. Baba took an active part in the struggle. During the Quit India movement of 1942, he organized lawyers to represent jailed nationalists and was himself thrown into prison.

A restless, dissatisfied, disturbed mind in search of the *raison d'etre* of life roused in him a wanderlust. During vacations he often wandered into the nearby jungles and villages. 'That microscopic look at village life taught me to hear the heartbeat of reality,' he recalled. He was appalled by the poverty, hunger, disease and deprivation that he witnessed all around. Besides learning of the plight of the downtrodden he also gained an overwhelming sense of the potentialities latent in the most humble and afflicted human beings. This faith in humanity has been one of the main springs of life and one of the principal reasons for his success in bringing out the best in the patients, workers, outcastes and even those rejected by their own people.

Young vagrant Murlidhar was as though engaged in a frantic search for something. He had an unquenchable zest for exploring and experimenting with all that there was in life. So he left no path untrodden, no stone unturned and no flavour unsavoured. From films to fashion to fast cars and from poetry to hunting, he tried and tested all. Dressed fashionably, he drove a Singer sports car with seats upholstered in tiger skin. He wrote poems and reviewed a column for the film magazine *The Cinegoer*. Through this magazine he made the great actresses Greta Garbo and Norma Shearer his pen friends. He fondly recalls a picture of Greta Garbo in a backless dress, which she had sent to him. 'Someone's stolen it, it used to hang right there,' he points to a spot on the wall.

Hunting became another passion with Baba during his youth. He read all available literature on it, as it was in him to throw himself whole-heartedly into anything he undertook. 'Then with gun in hand, he set out to become an accomplished hunter. Not wanting to use deceit in shooting wild animals, he started face-to-face encounters with them. Fearlessness being an innate trait, he never hesitated to challenge the animals from a short distance before shooting them. The hobby of hunting inevitably led to eating of flesh and drinking of spirits' *(The Man and His Mission).* About this period of his life Baba says:

> From my childhood, I have aspired to enjoy life every moment and to the fullest extent. I have seen and enjoyed both the dark and bright sides of life, its piety and sinfulness, the good and the bad, the most conventional and the wildest activities. In whatever I did, I aspired to ascend to the top and I never wanted thereafter to linger at the top of something when it was once reached. I instinctively realized that once the top is reached the process of descent and fall inevitably begins. I hunted the tiger not from a safe perch but facing him from the ground. When I drank, it was straight from the bottle and not in peg-measures. When I stopped, I never touched a drop thereafter. I ate non-vegetarian food every day, but when I realized that it amounted to 'the dead eating the dead', I gave it up permanently.

SADHNA ALIAS INDU

At thirty Murlidhar, being a practising lawyer and the son of a landlord, was considered a very eligible bachelor in his caste community and hence received many marriage proposals. But how could he marry? His mother's mental illness made him worry that no sane daughter-in-law would take on the challenge of living with and looking after an insane mother-in-law. So when the pressure of entering into matrimony from parents and close of kin mounted on him, he took up a vow of celibacy and left home to become an ascetic.

For two years he roamed around in search of the meaning of the self and the purpose of life. He trod the Himalayas, visited ashrams, met and conferred with ascetics and seers. But like Buddha he concluded that only self-denial and practising of rigorous rituals do not lead to emancipation. Involving oneself with the least and the lowest would lead to the understanding of the business of living. So he returned to be with those who needed him. Giving himself up for the search of the undefinable and otherworldly was a waste of life. He decided to dedicate himself to the service of those whose lives were not as blessed as his. His restlessness, his search for his true vocation had reached an end.

While attending the wedding of a distant relative, Baba met Indu Ghuleshastri (her maiden name). She belonged to a conservative Brahmin family of Sanskrit scholars. He spied her secretly helping the servants of the house in their menial chores. 'I thought no ordinary Brahmin girl would stoop to wash other people's clothes, when she could have been enjoying herself. And suddenly something inside me stirred,' he recalls. Her innocence and humane heart won his admiration and love. But he could not win the consent of Indu's parents when Baba asked for her hand in marriage. They objected to the vow of celibacy, the flowing beard and the saffron attire that Baba had adopted. Celibates don't marry! He must be a fraud. But in the end Baba's persistence and love for their daughter convinced Indu's parents and the marriage of affection and mutual consent took place on 18th December 1946. Baba was thirty two and Indu only twenty years at the time of marriage.

In marrying Baba, Indu, who was rechristened Sadhna, knew that she was marrying a man who lived an unconventional life and did not adhere to the codes of conduct practised by the Brahmin caste, whereas she was bred in an orthodox Hindu tradition by a family of gracious, reserved Sanskrit scholars. But she says, 'I never wanted to be an ordinary housewife. I wanted to marry someone who was different and daring. I used to see my sisters and friends who were living ordinary lives of cooking, cleaning and rearing children. I never wanted to be like them. I knew with this unusual man I would not be just a housewife.'

By the time of his marriage to Sadhna, Baba had already plunged himself into working with and for the sweepers, scavengers and other Harijan (lower castes) groups. In order to demonstrate empathy with the underprivileged, he had ceased to live in the farmhouse and lived in a thatched cottage instead. After marriage Sadhna went through a process of emotional and behavourial adjustment and relinquished her caste strictures against eating, drinking and living with Harijans. 'But... I have never regretted it. I chose this life and it has been a full and satisfying one,' she says.

In *The Man and His Mission*, S. M. Shirodkar and Dr. B.G. Bapat write:

> Till then she had only heard about Baba's work and superficially knew him. Now she got an opportunity to see his nature, his strict adherence to principles, his mass contacts, empathy with the poor, his untiring efforts to organize and awaken the downtrodden sections of society so as to win back their rights and justice and such other traits. Out of the eleven codes of behaviour which were emphasized and practised by Gandhi, adopted by him, she was witness daily to his un-attachment, indifference to taste in eating and drinking, use of only indigenous products and refusal to observe untouchability.
>
> She herself, being a strong-willed person, must have been mentally prepared to face all challenges, not to buckle under any crisis, to make untiring efforts, hearing praise and criticism with equanimity standing not only behind but shoulder to shoulder with him in all his projects and programmes. Her total involvement in Baba's heroic adventures showed her humility as well as determination in abundant measure. At one place she has said, 'I took keen interest in reading *Ramayana* and *Mahabharata* as a child. The spouse-worshipping women in these epics had become my ideal. This led to my later resolve to fully accept my husband's ideals. I still carry the gossamer burden of those ideals to this day and get happiness and get satisfaction from living by them.'
>
> Very soon, she had to face the worst challenge of her married life in

the form of Baba's *Shramashram* project, an extraordinary experiment of 'living as a commune' unique in contemporary history.

Sadhna Tai has written an unfinished biography, in which she relates the story of her early years with Baba (Chapter 4: 'Through Tai's Eyes').

MOTHER AVRILIA ALIAS SISTER LILA

Mother Gavrilia, born as Avrilia Papayani in Constantinople, was a member of the Orthodox Church of Greece and a trained physiotherapist who became well-known internationally for her unique talent as a spiritual guide. She had a dream in which she was instructed to go to India and serve the people there. She became the disciple of Guru Sivananda. At his ashram in Rishikesh she came to know of Baba Amte and his great work.

On New Year's Day in 1956, she met Baba at Anandwan. Her letters show great love and deep respect for him. Also one notices with admiration and perhaps some astonishment, the amazing spiritual affinity of these two persons from different regions and different countries.

Avrilia stayed in India for five years and travelled to many parts of the country. But with Baba Amte she shared a special relationship. The depth of this relationship is evident from the numerous letters that the two exchanged between 1956 and 1990 and also through the letters that Avrilia wrote to two of her closest friends, Helen Virvou and Yehuda, telling them all about Anandwan and Baba Amte.

In one such letter to Helen, she writes in great detail about her journey and first impression of Amte and Anandwan (Avrilia's biography *The Ascetic of Love* by Nun Gavrilia): 'The strange thing is that while man looks for divine inspiration in old and ruined temples, he fails to find it in human ruins.' This is what Avrilia was thinking as an ox-cart was taking her to Warora, through the jungle of central India. The night was very cold and she was freezing to the bone. She was wearing her only dress – a white summer garment, a doctor's-like blouse that was to become her uniform during her five-year stay in India. Without saying a word, the Indian ox-driver sitting next to her, covered her legs with a thick woolen blanket. He was probably doing the same for the sick of the colony, the lepers he carried to and from Anandwan. The going was rough and the night was very dark.

It was 1st January 1956. Her ministry to the lepers of India was to begin the following day. For the first time Avrilia stayed for two months at Anandwan. She wrote to Helen Virvou:

> In these two months I understood that there is much more to wonder at, to rescue and to love in the ruins of man, than in the most significant ruins of stone.... Courage, faith, patience, endurance and above all hope and joy can take root and blossom in the human heart, if it is given opportunity, if it is given love... The long hours of travelling by train had tired me much. The drive through the cold night did not help. But the moment I stepped into the temporary home of Baba Amte my weariness vanished and my spirit rejoiced at the simple, warm, homely atmosphere.
>
> There had been neither a formal salutation nor the typical western shaking of hands. The kind of smile on Baba Amte's face, as he came forward to meet me, spoke to my heart more than the warmest welcomes. All this time Mrs. Amte stood behind her husband, silent, holding a baby in her arms. The baby was not her own but the child of a leper woman of the colony and they were raising it in their home, together with their children, to save it from being contaminated by its mother. Their two boys were in bed at the time of the night.
>
> The following morning Baba Amte showed me around the settlement, explaining how it came into existence. Actually it was the story of his life. He started as a lawyer in Warora. During his tenure as Chairman of the Municipal Council, he became interested in social work. In order to learn more about the tasks and the working conditions of the municipal labourers, he himself worked for several months – even as a cleaner of public conveniences. One day while cleaning, he saw a man lying on the floor, his body covered with ulcers. The man was in the last stage of leprosy. Inspite of all the compassion he felt, he could not do anything. Like so many others, he bypassed the poor

man. But unlike others, he could not forget him. He could not chase from his mind what he had seen and understood, that he would not find peace and rest in his soul, unless he did something to relieve the pain and misery of the thousands of victims of this terrible disease, which the Indians havenamed so wisely '*Maharoga*'. That was eventually what brought Anandwan into existence. The government made a grant of some acres of land in the jungle and the project was started with donations by friends and acquaintances.

At first there were only a few patients, sheltered under a large tent... and a lame cow. Before he began his fight against leprosy, he had to fight against the natural conditions of the locality. The soil was swarming with snakes, scorpions and other such pests. His dogs were quite often snatched by tigers. They had to cut down trees, uproot bushes, clear the ground of rocks. Here was a task that demanded courage, faith, patience to the highest degree. Baba Amte and his co-workers were gifted with these three virtues.

Today the picture before the visitor's eye is entirely different. Instead of the jungle, green fields stretch around, producing what is necessary for the subsistence of the leper colony. Tents and sheds have been replaced by buildings. Cowsheds shelter 60 oxen and 40 cows, and the sale of milk yields a good income. In the early days, Baba Amte himself and his wife tended the animals. Now two cured lepers look after them.

At present the entire project is under the auspices of the Maharogi Sewa Samiti and has annexes in Warora and its environs. Today Anadwan has 112 inpatients and helps many thousands of outpatients every year. The number could be increased if adequate transport was available, but so far all requests have been turned down. Continuation of the good work is made possible, thanks to the patients' meagre contributions and donations made by friends.

Anandwan is not just a hospital for lepers. Here the sick are cured not only from the disease of the body, but also from the equally grave affliction of the soul that accompanies this terrible sickness; the feeling of utter loneliness, which is the outcome of social rejection and leads in turn to despair.

Not rarely, even cured lepers are rejected by their own family! One such case was that of the nurse assisting Baba Amte.

It is obvious that Avrilia had felt both deep respect and admiration in the presence of such dedication. Love and ministration had joined her to these people at once. In Anandwan she saw Christ in every leper, ministering to him every day, 'I came to India for no special reason. As you know the world is my home. All God's children, with no exception, interest me, not only the lepers,' she wrote to Baba from Delhi on 1st January 1956. She shared with the Amte family a friendship of great depth and spirituality. This is revealed by their correspondence between January 1956 and December 1990 and by the help she gave whenever her 'brother' faced a problem with his health (which he very often did due to the hard life he chose to follow), till 1971, when Baba Amte fell ill and had to be taken to London, for two weeks she spent the whole day at the hospital, sleeping at nights on a bench of the railway waiting room. She also often wrote about Vikas and Prakash, Amte's two dear sons, whom they had agreed she was to call Socrates and Plato. They must have felt the great love this Greek lady had for them, to be willing to accept this. When she first met them, they were 5 and 6 years old. She had much to do and the work was very demanding but somehow she found the time to teach them English. From her letters we learn that she continued to be interested in their schooling, as well as their university and postgraduate studies. This love never diminished. In a letter sent from Athens 16 years later in 1974, to her 'Socrates', by then Dr. Vikas, she wrote:

> To my mind when I think of India, your father represents the loving power energy of the country. Your mother represents the loving patience of the country and you represent its bright future. With your love for those patients you met as soon as you were able to know life, your heart got so united to them that I remember you as a little boy, wishing to be one of them – God forbid – so that you could mix with them and love them freely and fully.... You thank me because I taught you your first English lesson, but I must thank you instead. My teaching was not to help you. I loved you so much as a little boy – and still do – that I had to be able to talk one day with you. This was the only way.

Sister Lila, as Avrilia came to be known in India, visited many parts of India nursing the sick, teaching physiotherapy and speaking to large gatherings about the power of love. But wherever she went, Anandwan was always on her mind. Everywhere she went, at every step, with every old or new acquaintance, she tried and succeeded with God's help, to send to Anandwan all kinds of help. She took active interest in inspiring enthusiasm in hundreds of friends and acquaintances worldwide from this work. Her letters speak of tractors, jeeps, building materials, refrigerators, beds, mosquito nets, provisions, toys for the lepers' children and the nursery, medicines, cotton-wool, antiseptics, powdered milk. They contain names of Americans and Europeans she recommended and directed to Anandwan – to make this great work known the world over. She made contacts and secured help from international organizations such as the W.H.O., UNICEF and the International Red Cross.

From one of Baba's letters, written on 25th October 1961, one can understand in greater depth the love that the lord had placed in her soul for this great work. In this letter he writes to his dear Sister Lila about the contributions received:

> Beloved Sister, dreams are not horses to come running. If only my dear active sister had remained in India, they would have materialized... only you go around, in the villages and cities... please come back to your family... your brother needs your inspiration, your message. Come to Anandwan and fill us with your blessings.

Sister Lila left India for the monastic life in Bethany on 4th August 1959. Before leaving she sent the Amtes her last letter from India.

> When you get this letter I shall be, God willing, in Jerusalem. I fly tomorrow to Karachi, then to Beirut and around noon of the next day will reach Jerusalem.... How I feel our parting.... Some day I am sure god will make us meet. I shall always remember the farewell of the

> patients in Anandwan. Let love shine forever through all of you, Socrates, Plato, Renuka, Virili, above all Sadhana! —Your Sister Lila.

Sister Lila passed away peacefully in her sleep in 1990, in Greece, after having travelled to many countries offering physical and spiritual guidance to all those who needed it.

CHAPTER 3

From Law to Labour

In 1936, after acquiring his law degree from the Government Law College at Nagpur, Murlidhar started legal practice at Durg, as a junior to the then ex-member of the Legislative Assembly and a leading advocate Mr. Tamaskar. When Tamaskar got jailed during the independence struggle, Murli began working on his own. However, he soon became disgruntled with the attitude and behaviour of the clients, pleaders, as well as witnesses in criminal cases. He was disturbed by the fact that he was expected to defend those who had committed heinous crimes and, if they were acquitted, join them in a celebration. 'The whole thing was so repugnant,' he recalled. The result of handling criminal cases was that he became restless and ill at ease. 'He resolved not to take up briefs in which he had to lie,' Dr. Bharati, his daughter-in-law, recounts with a smile. Perceiving his son's discomfort, the elder Amte advised him to deal only in civil cases.

Another reason for the practice of law not being fully satisfying to young Murlidhar was the value, as measured by remuneration, that society attached to different kinds of work people did. As a lawyer, for instance, he worked short hours and earned a handsome salary, while labourers worked very hard for twelve hours a day and earned hardly enough for them to keep themselves and their dependants alive. This fact was incompatible with his finer sensibilities and hence a cause of much distress to him.

Disappointed, he returned to his home town Warora in 1940, with the intention of apparently making a new beginning there.

At Warora, he launched a new experiment of practising law on a cooperative basis jointly with two Englishmen, Mr. Swan and Mr. Christie, as his partners. This marked the beginning of Baba's experiment of cooperative living. These three lawyers maintained a joint bank account from which anyone could withdraw any amount at any time.

In Warora, Amte's youthful energy also found expression in various activities which he undertook out of his concern for the neglected and downtrodden. He helped occupational groups like weavers, sweepers and scavengers to organize themselves. He was clear in his mind about the need for such unions, as he believed that no unorganized, neglected section of society could get and enjoy its dues without unionization. He came to be actively associated with about sixteen organizations.

While tending to the family estates, Amte also became aware of a distinct uneasiness in himself about the social inequalities that were visible all around him. In the book *A Journey from Sympathy to Empathy*, the authors write that Baba observed 'that the tenants who cultivated the family's land in Goraja were poor and lived in squalor while he, the son of the landlord, lived in a comfortable farmhouse. He asked himself why, he, who had never planted a seed, should live in comfort, while the tenants who did everything should live in poverty.' In an attempt to ameliorate this injustice Amte stopped staying in the farmhouse when he visited his family, choosing instead to live in a thatched cottage. Though this did little to alter the state of the poverty-stricken tenants, it did demonstrate empathy with them, as it was the abnegation of a privilege.

In the 1940s Murlidhar also became drawn towards the independence movement. He had close contacts with the Indian Revolutionary Party, and at one time, he was even smuggling arms for them. There is a story that he was once going to be arrested for this gun-running activity but his mother's clever move saved him. There were some weapons kept in a pillow on a bed in the house. When the police were searching the house, his mother casually sat on the cot next to the pillow and diverted the attention of the police to other things. His contacts with the revolutionaries made him a believer in armed struggle but soon he realized that their philosophy would not lead to a social revolution. While he still believed that an armed struggle could be instrumental in winning independence, he was convinced that it would never lead to all-round progress. Realizing the limitations of the armed struggle, Amte turned to Gandhi's path of constructive nation building.

In 1942 Gandhi launched the Quit India movement and Amte, like millions of youth under Gandhi's spell, joined the movement. He courted arrest and was imprisoned for raising the slogan *Vande Mataram*. This inner turmoil and transition began affecting Amte's lifestyle too. Expensive clothes were replaced by rough, inexpensive khadi and a manual spinning wheel adorned his abode. He began religiously practising the eleven codes of conduct, as preached and practised by Gandhi, in addition to regularly visiting the Ashrams of Gandhi and Vinoba Bhave.

In 1942, after release from prison, he plunged himself into fighting a political case. The Mahar Regiment of the army placed in Chimur had committed atrocities against the local people. Following the protest raised by the Indian National Congress, there was a commission appointed to investigate the case. C. Rajgopalachari, K.M. Munshi and Murlidhar Amte were the pleaders on behalf of the local people. Amte undertook the full responsibility of pleading the case, as the other two gentlemen were preoccupied with various issues related to the freedom struggle. As a part of his involvement in the freedom movement, he organized the lawyers of Warora for giving free legal service to political prisoners for defending their cases in court.

Around this period Amte had an interesting experience. 1942 was the year of the Second World War, and the British army was moving extensively through all parts of the country. A carriage was reserved in all trains for the soldiers, but they were also allowed to travel in other carriages along with the civilians. On one occasion, Amte was travelling from Warora to Nagpur and a group of British soldiers happened to be his fellow-travellers. A newly-married couple, a young Tehsildar and his wife, too were seated in the same compartment. The young shy bride became the focus of attention for the soldiers, who began teasing her with boorish and vulgar comments. The husband was too frightened to defend his wife so that the lady, though unable to bear the teasing, had to keep mum. Amte rose chivalrously and raised a strong protest against the teasing, but his protests fell on deaf ears. However, this led to an argument between Amte and the soldiers, which soon turned into a physical tussle. Though Amte's early experiences as an amateur wrestler had stood him in good stead, he could not prevail against the collective muscle power of the group for long. He was beaten badly and thrown out of the compartment. But he was not one to give up the fight easily. He did not allow the train to leave the platform till he got an assurance from the Commandant of the soldiers' unit, who had to be summoned to the spot to settle the issue. On hearing of the incident, Gandhi expressed his appreciation by naming Murli 'Abhay Sadhak Amte' (Fearless Achiever).

On 18th December 1946, the 'Abhaya Sadhak' married his soul mate Indu. 'Marriage erected a protective stockade around my restless wandering,' he recalls. By the time of his marriage Amte had shed most of the caste practices fondly cherished by Brahmins. He mingled freely with the Harijans and had no qualms as regards eating from Harijan homes. The process of Indu's initiation into Amte's unconventional lifestyle began slowly, she being brought up in an orthodox Hindu household.

By now Amte was completely under the influence of Gandhi and Vinoba's ideology, along with communist and socialist philosophy. 'Marx, Prince Kropotkin, Ruskin, Kumarappa had possessed my mind,' says he. In the course of his reading he was coming across ideas such as *Sarvodaya* (welfare of all the poor), dignity of labour, fair wages, exploitation of labour by vested interests, etc. As an answer to these, the organizing of labour unions appealed to him as a way out, which led to his fraternizing with sweepers, scavengers and other low-caste groups. He became president of the scavengers' union. On the basis of his mass contacts, he also got elected to the local municipal committee and became its vice-president. This coincided with India achieving her independence in 1947 as well as the birth of Vikas, Amte's first-born.

Here it is essential to understand Amte's conformity to communist and socialist ideologies because he is often misunderstood to be a typical labour leader. But the truth is that he never owed complete allegiance to any 'ism' or philosophy. Rather, he picked the practical and humane aspects of any school of thought that appealed to his own beliefs. 'You don't become Moses by parroting the ten commandments. We are all doing this parroting, "Marx said this, Lenin said that." My God! The problem cannot be resolved by elimination of a class. The leaders of Russia and China came from the soil, yet the worst atrocities have been perpetrated not by capitalists but by labourers who have come to power. They have not answered the basic question, that of how to build a man,' says Amte. He did not expect unions to fight exclusively for financial gains, dissociated from the socio-political scene. He could never agree to the idea of monetary gains being the exclusive motivation and guiding thought of the labour movement. Here he was in total agreement with Marx's thought that under a capitalistic society, labour has no escape from financial exploitation unless they got organized. Marx insisted that labour unions should not forget their historical role of ending the wage-system and slavery to wage scales. But he also cautioned, 'They ought not to forget that they are fighting with effects but not with the causes of these effects; that they are retarding the downward movement, but not changing its direction; that they are applying palliatives, not curing the malady.'

Marxism is fundamentally concerned with labour. 'Labour is the source of all wealth, the political economists assert. And it really is the source – next to nature, which supplies society with the material that it converts into wealth. But it is infinitely more than this. It is the prime basic consideration for all human existence and this to such an extent that, in a sense, we have to say that labour created man himself'. After studying Marx,

Ruskin and the others, he concluded that 'labour is capable of the alchemy of converting dust into gold' and agreed with the philosophy propounded by Gandhi and Vinoba that 'Labour purifies the soul.' It was clear that Amte wanted to accord its rightful place to labour rather than use labour unions as a tool for class conflicts.

Since Amte was the president of the scavengers' union, visits to their hutments were frequent. Indu accompanied her husband on most of the visits. There was a day when she drank water for the first time from a Harijan home, and from that day the barriers that religious orthodoxy had built between her and the so-called untouchables began to crumble.

The process entailed both learning and unlearning – learning to view human beings in a new light, which meant unlearning the traditional ways that had built up barriers, separating different sections of society. However, the Amtes' fraternizing with sweepers, scavengers and other untouchable groups was frowned upon by the high caste Hindus. The couple was, hence, given a notice to leave the rented house, which was owned by a Brahmin. At this juncture, one of Amte's friends, Mr. R.K. Patil, offered him timely assistance by placing at his disposal a house and the surrounding property of 7 acres. Here, in their new abode, Amte and Indu went ahead with their idea of inter-caste community living. It was a unique experiment. Scavengers, cobblers, Mahars, bamboo-weavers, middle-class white-collar employees, professionals, Hindus, Muslims, men, women and children from different classes and different occupations were brought together in a group of 15–20 persons. This formed the *Shramashram* (workers' hermitage), which was open to all, irrespective of caste, creed or occupation. Each was expected to share the earnings and the work of running the place. And the motto of the *Shramashram* was to be 'Shram hi hai Shri Ram hamara' (Work is Lord Ram for us). While Murli took upon himself such tasks as splitting wood, carrying baskets of vegetables grown on the premises on his head to sell in the local market, tilling the land, keeping accounts, etc. Indu performed such duties as nursing the sick, carrying water from the well, cooking, cleaning and attending to guests. The ashram was run on the basis of sharing – sharing of cultivating the land, maintenance, earnings, problems, and sorrows and joys of all the twenty people.

Meanwhile Amte continued his involvement with the various labour unions that he had organized. During his tenure as the vice-chairman of the Warora Municipality and chairman of the scavengers' union, there was a crisis, which left a chain of events in its trail. The scavengers went on a strike, demanding better conditions and wages. When he talked with them they questioned, 'Will you be able to do the dirty work we are doing daily? If you carry the nightsoil on a rainy day, you will know what our work is like.' Amte accepted the challenge and worked as a scavenger, not for a day or two, but for the next nine months, cleaning 40 latrines a day! The motive behind Amte's taking on the challenge was not mere bravado, but a genuine desire to have a first-hand feel of the plight of the scavengers. He would be up at 3 a.m. every day and devote four hours, from 4 a.m. to 8 a.m. to scavenging and the rest of his time he divided between pursuing his legal practice and the *Shramashram* project.

For a year and a half the *Shramashram* project was kept going mostly through the efforts of the Amtes, but after that, unfortunately, due to various reasons the project had to be abruptly ended. According to Indu, 'The commune disintegrated due to epidemics and financial constraints.' However, even in its failure the experiment in community living had given Amte a vision for the years to follow. 'I could see the vision of emancipation and creativity through labour,' he asserted.

CHAPTER 4

Through Tai's Eyes

Stepping from an austere and tradition-bound arena into Murli's unconventional realm must have left the young Indu completely bewildered. Yet she was up for the challenge and before long made a triumphant transition, from an orthodox Indu to a liberal Sadhana (as she came to be renamed after marriage). Not only did she successfully adopt her husband's lifestyle, but also ardently participated in all of Murli's efforts in alleviating the pain and suffering of the social outcasts. As a result of the love and care she tendered to all those who came to the Amte doorstep in various stages of sufferings, she came to be fondly called 'Tai' (aunt) by everyone. And for the same reason Murli was rechristened 'Baba' (father). More than half a century later, Sadhana Tai had a rich repository of recollections, which she began recording in the form of an autobiography. Even though the autobiography remains unfinished, it is the best source of information about the courtship and marriage of Murli and Sadhana, elucidating various aspects of the former's personality. What follows is the story of Baba Amte in Sadhana Tai's words.

* * *

There's a world of difference between the Sadhana after marriage and the earlier Indu Ghule (her maiden name). Whenever I remember my past, I am amazed at the change that has taken place. While passing through life as it develops, this change has occurred naturally without my being conscious about it.

I used to be very shy, unable to speak even to women, not to say men. When I did not speak a word to him, a friend of my father angrily said, 'Indu's words, like gold, are worth Rs. 80 a *tola*' (those days that was the price of gold), and this was not untrue. I mixed freely with small children but never went anywhere near adults. My mother used to call me a dumb doll. I have suffered in various ways because of my awkwardness. I was incapable of getting anything done outside my house. A telling example of my extreme shyness was when my heart began to palpitate at the time of receiving the annual prize for my first rank at the school prize-distribution ceremony. It was an ordeal for me to climb the stage to accept the prize. I used to then wish that I had not stood first. I was not even distantly acquainted with boldness. Because of my shyness I would not refuse anything that people would ask me to do.

Because of this nature, I could not enjoy college life. Not only had I no male friends, but I did not have even a single female friend. Having been educated in a boys' school, I had no childhood girlfriends either. Against this background, isn't it a surprise that I had a love marriage and that too with an unusual person?

In those days, my only knowledge about spinning wheel, khadi, nationalist movement, etc. was through what I had heard. Ours was a very orthodox, religious and tradition-bound family. The religious scholarship in our family had been handed down for seven generations. I had deeply imbibed these traditions. I observed all rites, rituals, fasts, segregationist edicts to the last detail. I had a very pious mind. Even if I did some injustice to somebody unknowingly, my mind could never be at ease till I had made amends.

I took a very active part in celebrating all religious festivals and was more devout in observing those rites which women traditionally performed for their husbands. It is as clear as daylight that at present I am enjoying the fruits of this piety. However much Baba may deride it, I stand firmly on my convictions.

I lost my father when he was only forty. Thus, I was deprived of fatherly affection at my eighth year. In the absence of my father, my mother had to shoulder the entire burden of the family when she was only thirty. As all her elder children were daughters, she had none to turn for succour. Several strict restrictions were imposed on all of us girls so as to protect the family's image and honour. We could attend no meetings, visit no cinema theatres and had to be accompanied by some responsible adult escorting us to the school or college. We did not attend classes when there was no escort available. In those days, being girls was treated as a crime. There was a total prohibition against reading novels, dramas or stories. There was no way to know what was happening in the world around us. We were expected to do the household chores, be hospitable to guests and, time permitting, catch up with our studies. It does not mean that we were straitjacketed. There was enough scope for fun. I proved very helpful to my mother in doing the daily household chores. Our intimacy was such that she used to say, 'Indu is my right hand.' Even without being instructed or even before my mother could think of some chore, I would have finished it, surprising her and winning her approbation. This was my habit, and this continues to this day. However, Baba does not easily give me a pat on my back but manages to find some fault. Publicly, however, he appreciates me, though I do not aspire for such public appreciation.

In spite of such a unique nature that I had, isn't it a wonder that a public man like Baba could be attracted towards me? Temperamentally, Baba is very sociable while I am fond of solitude; Baba likes to speak while I am very reticent, having never climbed a stage. Baba is an artist while I have no affinity for any art; Baba has his head in the clouds while my feet are firmly planted on the ground. The 'dream bride' he might have imagined in youth comes nowhere near me, yet, the rough cotton thread of Baba (no doubt, he is an expert in using the most delicate thread to reach the skies) got very smoothly interwoven with my silky one (my father was a dealer in silk cloth) to make such a beautiful tapestry as to attract the attention of a very large number of people.

My life stream was flowing placidly when Baba appeared suddenly and threw a big stone in it. The stream got disturbed for a while and this resulted in a number of people related to me becoming restless.

My elder sister was yet to be married, and hence there was no question of finding a match for me. Even so, I could realize that I was much coveted by many young men. On the plea that my elder sister was yet to be married and so my case was out of reckoning, quite a few suitors had to be displeased and disappointed. At around this time, my mother's uncle, who was married to Baba's sister, called him for help in arranging and fixing my elder sister's marriage as the proposed groom was a close friend of Baba.

Baba arrived at our place with a flowing beard, long tresses of matted hair covering his back, a cane staff in hand, a cloth bag as his only luggage and a rough woolen rug on his shoulder. From behind the door, we were looking at him and making fun of him as a 'staff-carrying ascetic'. We were quite accomplished in poking fun at others. As a sign of his determination to observe celibacy, Baba had adopted this tactic, but it proved to be a dishonest gambit (though till then he was extraordinarily honest!).

Just then, my mother came in laughing and said to us, 'Did you see Amte's Murli and his buffoonery?' Her voice was tinged with sadness. Soon thereafter, her uncle invited us out and introduced each of us to Baba. While introducing me, he lavishly praised me for my expertise in household chores and for being the topper of my class. Baba was looking at me and for a moment our eyes met. True to my nature, my eyes turned down. While I was being praised, Baba was smiling. I became attracted to him notwithstanding his attire. I felt a great respect for him. It cannot be denied that simultaneously some unknown restlessness gripped my heart.

Just a few hours before Baba's arrival, I had been presented before the family of a prospective groom who had a Ph. D. I had shown my unwillingness to marry him and my maternal grandfather was extremely annoyed with me. He was trying to persuade me through others to change my mind. I hardly knew anything about Baba, but my mother and my grandfather mentioned to him casually as a respected outsider about my refusal. Equally casually he said, 'Leave it to me to find a suitable match for Indu. Have no worry.'

In connection with my elder sister's wedding, Baba was our houseguest for a week. I was nominated to look after the guests, their comforts and convenience and the entire responsibility for this had been vested in me. I took special care of Baba as a 'prominent' guest. But while attending him, I experienced a unique pleasure and enthusiasm. The whole house had become topsy-turvy during the marriage preparations and all rooms were badly disorganized. I did not know about Baba's habit of saying prayers. On the first day, he somehow managed to say his prayers amidst the chaos. I felt very ashamed and that very night, I prepared a room for his prayer, thoroughly cleaning it, organizing it and spreading a mat. Thereafter, my service and Baba's prayers continued undisturbed. I used to eavesdrop on his prayer, standing on the staircase. During those days, we hardly exchanged a word with each other, and that too in connection with some chore. We both, however, realized the galloping change taking place in our minds. Baba sought to attribute convenient meaning to the services I rendered, and I was not a fool not to understand the emotion conveyed by his eyes. It must be admitted that I was a very fast learner as far as that was concerned.

As a prank, my family members started teasing me alluding to Baba and his comic appearance. 'Amte', they said, 'would jump at a chance to marry Indu' and so on. However, when they had to face the truth, everybody was brutally shocked.

Baba came to our place once again, about a week after my sister's marriage. But this time there was no sign of his reserved nature. He used to boldly order me about. Once he gave all of us a long lecture on khadi. I could not understand this crafty duplicity. He had not till then disclosed his mind. I, however, was acutely distracted after Baba's first departure and became conscious of this change in me. But Baba's ascetic attire made even a thought of marrying him look objectionable and sinful. No doubt that an indefinable attraction had taken root.

This time Baba stayed for three days. He talked very little to me and that too in connection with some errand. He mainly talked to my mother and sisters. The family traditions precluded any dialogue between us. But by this time, he started taking a keen interest in the affairs of our family. After his return to Warora, a thick envelope containing a long letter for me was received. It was scandalous that such a letter came to me, but its receipt made me experience conflicting emotions: ecstasy for having received a letter from Baba and trauma that such a letter meant the breach of family traditions and norms. The person in whose hands it was delivered opened it as it was not addressed to me personally. It contained eulogistic references to me. I still possess that letter, since everyone is susceptible to praise. It paid tribute to my services, devotion to work and even beauty. I was watching the reaction of the family with bated breath. 'What has this celibate to do with Indu's beauty?' Is this why he was trying to find out everything about her?' and so on. Some of the relatives were even amused. Everybody was surprised that an ascetically attired celibate had written such a letter. There was no direct proposal of marriage. Feigning total ignorance about the hidden motive, I wrote a simple reply, that too after the family approved it. At the time of closing and sealing the envelope, however, I added 'yours' before my signature. This was enough indication for Baba, and thereafter a stream of letters, each more flowery than the previous one, started. As the family censored my replies, they were very formal. When I failed to reply to one or two of his letters due to apprehension, I received a blank sheet to convey his hurt. It was addressed as 'Dear Indu' and ended with 'yours alone Murli', with nothing in between. Being a slave to family norms, and for fear of playing with fire, I could not write before any relationship between us was formally approved. I passed those days in abject frustration, reading and re-reading the letters that I had received. During this period, Baba once came to us at Nagpur and claimed that I had misconstrued his letters. My mother was an extremely credulous person and ordered me to pay my respects to him. I had to prostrate before him and Baba used the occasion to drop the rough woollen rug, carried on his shoulder, on me as if accidentally, convincing me that his public actions were a mere sham.

On his return to Warora, however, there was a flood of love letters and an unequivocal proposal of marriage. Then a council was held at our place. When asked, I readily gave my consent. That made everybody sour-faced. Several efforts were made and inducements were offered by relatives to dissuade me from my decision, because in the marriage market those days, I was in great demand. Baba's age, looks, vows, all posed different problems. Sometimes I became so restless that I once wrote to Baba expressing my inability to control the developments, releasing him from his promise to me and so on. He was shocked, but the impact of the atmosphere in which I had grown was so strong upon me that I couldn't even dream of rebellion.

It is no mean surprise how this emotion, which totally changed the course of his life, entered his mind. He had taken a vow to remain celibate throughout his life.

It is equally surprising that I decided to marry Baba against the wishes of all. This was probably due to my eagerness to live an unconventional life. It is also true that love was born in the very first meeting. I often lent a helping hand to the old maid servant of our family to clean the pots and pans. Similarly, when many untouchable women came to the public water tap opposite our home, and had to wait for long hours till somebody would give them water (the untouchables were prohibited from touching the tap or taking water directly), I took pity on them and ensuring that nobody was around, I called them to the back of our compound and filled their containers with the water from our well. In such deeds, it never dawned on me that I was doing something great; it had become my second nature. Baba, however, found these deeds to be out of the ordinary. So, he learnt everything about me from the maid servant and my mother and then only took his final decision. I did not however, make any inquiries about him. I was immensely taken in by his loving, compassionate nature. The lover in him is immortal.

On 9th August, our match was finalized, and 18th December 1946 was decided as the date for the wedding ceremony. The intervening period of four months helped us know each other better.

Baba's well-wishers, who rejoiced at the news of Baba's forthcoming wedding, called on me to offer me their good wishes. Out of many who did so, I recall the names of Mr. R.K. Patil, Dr. Barlinge, Kamlatai Hospet, Mohoni brothers and Mr. H.V. Kamath. I looked younger than my age then and was always clad in silk saris with rich brocade and it was but natural that everybody felt concerned about how I would be able to adjust to a khadi-clad tramp like Baba. However, each one of them was happy that Baba was settling down to a married life.

The four months' period preceding marriage was very memorable. At that time, there were no pressures, except eager waiting for the union. Even today, if we are separated for a few days, we experience the same keen longing for each other.

Eight to ten days before the wedding date, Baba came to Nagpur and stayed with our family. We chit-chatted till midnight. Thereafter, Baba was lying on his bed on the upper floor with doors to the room wide open. Just then, some burglars entered the horse. Baba caught one of them and held him tightly. Baba was extensively stabbed with a big knife and was bleeding profusely. Before others climbed the stairs, the thieves had escaped. Baba had been seriously wounded and his eye was saved by a whisker. He was removed to the Mayo hospital for treatment. Baba was determined not to miss the wedding date. He took part in the ceremony with plasters and bandages all over the body. About this, Baba has said, 'I performed the marriage rites with plaster-covered body. The treating physicians had warned me that there was not much hope that I would survive. Even then, both of us were determined to get married and then one day, I wrote to her in a letter, "Let us live in such a way that every moment will become a day and every day a lifetime." ' The marriage ceremony was performed on 18th December 1946.

We never realized how the time between 9th August and 18th December flew. The ecstasy of that time was unique. After the marriage, we stayed in the Dharampeth bungalow for a month. During this period I visited my paternal home only once.

It was the beginning of February and Baba was seized with

thoughts of Warora. Many of his well-wishers were eagerly awaiting our arrival. I had painted a mental picture about life at Warora. As the train was speeding towards Warora, my mind was rushing to that town hundred times faster. Future brought about an admixture of the colours with which I had painted life there and it became multi-hued like a rainbow.

We reached Warora. Baba's friends had planned to take us home in a procession accompanied by a band of musicians but on learning that Baba was opposed to this idea, they dropped the plan. We were no more a newly-married couple. On entering our home, I was overcome by a feeling of satisfaction for having arrived at 'my home' with independence, a sense of inner peace and ownership and I heaved a sigh of contentment. It did not have the appearance of a family home but was a bachelor's quarter full of chaos. The piteous condition of several things indicated that a human hand had not touched them for long years. They appeared to me to be pining for my arrival.

Several visitors came to make solicitous inquiries. The sudden change in Baba's life had aroused a sense of curiosity and elation in the minds of all.

We cooked our dinner together. This marked the beginning of the practice of doing everything jointly. Baba is quite adept in doing all jobs normally performed by the menfolk in the house as well as those that traditionally women handle. He never fights shy of doing womanly chores. The unique taste of a meal cooked by both of us together in our own rightful home is no more found in our hectic life today. The flame of love enkindled in me and Baba's all-pervading compassion brightened our lives and instilled in us a new spirit.

On the third day after our arrival, the Harijans (people of the Scheduled Castes) took the initiative to arrange a reception for us in the colony. Those days, Baba was the leader of Harijans. There were only very few persons from higher castes who attended it. Several leaders of the Harijan community felicitated Baba and some elders gave him their blessings. In an emotionally charged reply, Baba thanked all of them. Both of us sat on a dais which was ornately decorated. They presented us with silver etchings of Gandhiji and Netaji Subhash Chandra Bose. We had not accepted any marriage gifts till then but could not refuse these trinkets the poor people presented from the bottom of their heart.

Till then, I had rigidly stuck to the norms of behaviour ordained for the Brahmins and had not accepted even a glass of water from non-Brahmins. At my ancestral home, we had to change all our clothes if, by oversight, we touched a person belonging to any scheduled caste. This often happened in the case of fruit vendors, who were mostly Harijans. I got down from the dais and went and sat amongst the Harijan women. According to their custom, all of them cracked their knuckles over my head to ward of any evil eye. Many of those women were latrine cleaners. Accustomed to the inhuman treatment they got from the society, they started moving away from me. They were afraid of polluting me by their touch as I was a Brahmin. Without any hesitation or reservation, I freely mixed with them. This absolutely floored them. Some of them asked me whether on going home I would have a bath and change my clothes (To wash off the pollution caused by their touch). I solemnly assured them that I shall not do so. They were quite surprised and this took me closer to them. Thereafter, every day a few Harijan women came in their spare time, and I and Baba's younger sister started teaching them the alphabet.

On coming to know about Harijans entering our house, the landlord gave us a notice to vacate.

Every evening we went to the Harijan settlement. Baba carried books containing nationalist songs. We sung many of them and got the residents there to memorize them. It became our routine to visit the settlement, and that caused a number of tongues to wag. Baba tried to make them aware of their rights. He used to talk to them about the atrocities committed upon the untouchables by the higher castes and by the rich upon the poor. Many people got aroused by these speeches. Many of them got busy organizing a cleanliness drive within the settlement. Wrestling arenas were started. The people there started worshipping Baba. This led others to accuse Baba of being a communist, suspecting that Baba was engaged in provoking them.

Criticisms grew frequent. But they had no effect on Baba. The next step Baba initiated was to open tea stalls and eating-houses in the town to the Harijans. One day Baba entered a restaurant accompanied by one man each belonging to the communities of scavengers, Mahars, cobblers, Mangs and Buruds. The owner was stunned to see Baba accompanied by these five-six untouchables. Reluctantly he served them tea in regular cups, but later on he kept these cups aside. Baba started playing this havoc in one eatery every day on the pretext of a constitutional. This started a spate of threats of physical violence on him and even our house was intermittently pelted with stones at night.

We had our ancestral titles to land in the village Goraj, five miles from Warora. The institution of landlords who possess titles to large tracts of land has now become history. We decided to pay the village a visit. People used to come to know as if by wireless transmission that the landlord is coming with his bride for a visit, and large groups of people stood waiting at several places. Their faces showed an extraordinary curiosity. They were curious to set their eyes on the bride of an ascetic vowed to celibacy. I became extremely shy with the awareness that everyone in the crowd was staring at me like a museum piece and was extremely anxious to get away from it all. If there were any oldies in the crowd, Baba would order me to prostrate before them as obeisance to old age without any consideration for caste, creed, religion or status. I thus prostrated before several old Muslims also.

They gave me a new insight. I never hesitated to bow before any old people, whatever be their status or community, though as the wife of the village landlord this was not expected of me. Some win the hand of blessing of the Goddess of wealth, some the Goddess of erudition, but we both were receiving innumerable blessings of goodwill. We credited all these into the fixed deposit account for our future welfare. They have steered the boat of our life safely all these years through all calamities.

Before his marriage, Baba was held in these villages in exceptional awe, thanks to his flowing beard, matted hair and cane staff. In the past, he had educated the villagers through programmes of early morning marches, devotional music, drives to clean the roads and compounds and chanting of the holy name on the lines of Saint Tukdoji (a nationalist ascetic, who became very famous on account of his relentless drives of mass awakening). Thus everything was proceeding in an orderly fashion. But my presence disturbed the rhythm. Earlier, no woman showed the courage to talk to Baba directly, and the ignorant, illiterate women took Baba's celibacy as an indication of his misogyny and refrained from even stretching out their saris to dry anywhere near the path Baba was to walk on. Thus Baba's ego had been very well pampered here. My presence gave them the license to talk freely and even tease us.

On evening walks, we used to go well beyond the village boundary. The elders used to admonish us because it would get quite late in the evening by the time we returned. 'Why do you loiter for so long? She is a new bride, several trees are inhabited by ghosts and spirits. Why take her with you (at such a time)?' They honestly felt worried. These were the days of 1946.

* * *

Unfortunately, Tai's autobiography, which would have given us a more subtle understanding of Baba the man, his mission and motivation, could not be completed by Tai due to her and Baba's failing health and their overworked schedule. Yet she has not given it up entirely. She still hopes to take it up again from where she left it.

CHAPTER 5

Anandwan – How It All Began

He had a dream. A dream wherein he saw the wonders that he could perform for the despised, forsaken, shunned lepers of the country. If nobody would lend a helping hand to these fingerless ones, if everybody hated to see these eyeless ones, he, Murlidhar Devidas Amte, would show the way. And he did. With just faith. A faith that moved mountains and made everyone believe. He started off ploughing a lonely furrow, but invariably found a large following later.

Whatever may have been the actual reasons for the failure of Baba's *Shramashram* project, he does not recount them. He explains the failure by drawing analogies and creating allegories with the facility of a poet, 'It is wrong to evaluate an adventure in terms of ultimate success or failure. An adventurer does not bother about success or failure. Some experiments succeed, others fail. The small failures will be the launching pads of bigger adventures, just as the failure of *Shramashram* led to the success of Anandwan. "Victory is achieved by those who fight and overcome failures," it is the lesson taught by history. The germ of success is hidden within every failure. Such failures can be compared to the few steps a leopard retreats before pouncing on his prey. Very often the failure marks the turning point from the wrong to the right direction.'

'I treat my capacity to forget failures as my biggest strength, a blessing of nature. Though such failures may evoke derisive laughter, they do not bring disappointment, remorse or take my breath away through setbacks. These small failures help me find the right direction,' says Baba.

It was while working as a scavenger that Baba had an experience that gave a firm direction to his life. One rainy evening, as he walked home after a hard day's work, he came across a huddled figure, lying like a heap of discarded rubbish in a gutter. At first it seemed like a bundle of rags. On investigation, he found that it was not only a man terribly stricken with leprosy but also alive. The man was named Tulsiram. Tulsiram's face was almost entirely decayed, his body swarmed with maggots and the stench emanating from his rotting flesh was overpowering. He lay on the ground gasping for breath.

Recalling the time Baba says, 'I saw a man in the ultimate stages of leprosy, a rotting mass of human flesh, with two holes in the place of a nose, without trace of fingers or toes and with worms in the sores that had once been nostrils and eye sockets.'

Horrified at the sight, terrified of infection, with a retching stomach he ran from the scene in fear, throwing a piece of cloth on the 'thing'. But he could not run away from the feeling of self-loathing that began to hound him once he was safely within the confines of his comfortable dwelling. The memory of the ghastly sight of the dying leper relentlessly haunted him. The moment of epiphany came later when that gruesome sight was recollected in tranquility. And what vexed him most was how he had reacted: the revulsion and fear that overcame him at the sight of Tulsiram. How could he have left a lonely, forsaken man to lie alone in the rain?

There were a zillion fears that Baba had banished by then. He recalled his feelings, 'I thought I was not afraid of anything. Because I fought British Tommies to save the honour of an Indian lady, Gandhiji called me "Abhay Sadhak", a fearless seeker of truth. When the sweepers of Warora challenged me to clean gutters, I did so. And here I was running away from a dying man. This fear, I knew I had to crucify, to get rid of.' He forced himself to return to the rotting, dying Tulsiram. He put up a bamboo awning to shield the man from rain, gave him food and tended to his wounds. Three days later Tulsiram died in Baba's arms.

That man Tulsiram irrevocably changed Baba's life. He had always thought of himself as being fearless and daring. However, the whole Tulsiram episode shattered this self-image. The very sight of the dying leper filled him with irrepressible dread. Even as he cared for the man, the fear did not leave him. For the next six months, after the passing away of Tulsiram, he lived with the unrelenting agony of this crisis. He writes about it thus:

> A person mentally grasps the currents and counter-currents in the life around him. Many impulses, emotions, ideas, thought processes take shape, and then comes an explosive moment. For instance, one Baba Amte is performing the service of carrying a basket of night soil on his head and is confronted by a devastated leprosy patient lying in the gutter in his path. A universal suffering in the shape of that patient pierces his conscience like a hurricane and for a while everything becomes blank. In the radiation caused by that implosion, his social service, practice of fearlessness, evening prayers, *Shramashram*, wife, children, everything loses the meaning of its existence. The process, however, doesn't stop there. A new equilibrium emerges from it and a new shape takes place and Anandwan emerges.

Baba was so deeply affected by his experience with Tulsiram that he developed an acute sense of his own vulnerabilities, such as the possibility of one of his family members contracting the disease.

> Thereafter (after the experiment of *Shramashram*) at a street corner, I saw the shattered form of a human being full of maggots in the eyes, while carrying a basket of night soil on my head! At that moment, I experienced the piercing thorns of fear that I had never experienced while fighting the knives of attackers or shooting a pouncing tiger. I sheltered the oozing body of that leprosy patient from the pouring rain. That moment began my real struggle for fearlessness. Though I reached home with the false emotional satisfaction of having given the diseased some warmth by covering him with a piece of hessian cloth, I could not wipe off the picture from my mind. The only question, the only thought that gripped my mind was, 'What if my wife or children

> suffered from this disease?' I kept on thinking (and realized that) love cannot exist where there is fear. And if there is no love, can God be there? How can I call myself a practitioner of fearlessness? To overcome this fear and to eradicate it from public mind, I involved myself in this work.

This was the moment of truth, of revelation, in Baba's life, which finally led to a decision that changed the entire course of his life thereon. Baba, then thirty four, decided to dedicate himself to the care and rehabilitation of leprosy patients. 'That is why I took up leprosy work. Not to help anyone but to overcome that fear in my life. That it worked out good for others is a byproduct. But the fact is that I did it to overcome fear,' he maintained.

'We see beauty in the devastated relics of Ajanta and Ellora caves,' says Baba, 'Why should we not see the beauty in the disfigured human bodies? Why should such disfigurement terrify us? I started my leprosy work to find answers to all these questions,' he added.

First the failure of the *Shramashram* project and then the encounter with Tulsiram, which brought a moment of intense soul-searching and realization. Baba realized he had reached the end of one phase of life and also saw the beginning of another, even more challenging phase ready to be taken up.

Even though he was resolute in pursuing his mission of serving the leprosy-afflicted, he understood that the task at hand was monumental. He was in no way deterred or intimidated by the work he had taken upon his shoulders. But it was not easy, he very well knew in his heart. He had a wife and child (young Vikas) and there was the severe social prejudice against the disease. But Sadhana Tai supported him all the way: 'You must follow the dictates of your heart. I shall find my happiness in following you.'

Once the decision was made, Baba set himself a number of goals with regard to this work. First, he had to give up his lucrative practice as a lawyer. He could not continue his participation in public life because the mission he was undertaking was like a leap into the unknown that would demand all his time, money and efforts. Therefore, he disengaged himself from all the organizations with which he was actively associated.

He needed to know more about leprosy as a disease, its treatment and prevention, so he began reading about it and about all those who had rendered pioneering service in its eradication. But he also realized that this was not enough, he had to have first-hand experience of treating leprosy patients.

Arrangements existed for training of leprosy workers at the leprosy home started at Dattapur by Mr. Manohar Diwan, the renowned Indian pioneer of leprosy work, which he had undertaken with the blessings of Gandhi and Vinoba. Baba started working two days per week in the leprosy asylum at Dattapur, on the advice of Vinoba Bhave. For this he had to travel to Dattapur from Warora via Wardha during these two days every week. On the basis of the experience gained at Dattapur, Baba opened a diagnosis-cum-treatment centre at Warora, opposite the government hospital. A large number of leprosy patients started visiting it. According to BBC economist Graham Turner, 'Baba was busy from eight in the morning until late in the afternoon, diagnosing, giving injections, cleaning out ulcers with a knife, removing decomposing bones and dressing wounds.'

Since Baba had already given up his law practice, funds were meagre. There was a complete transformation in the Amte's lifestyle. Good clothes, good food, movies and fast cars were all things of a vague, distant past. 'We had no milk, no curds and no broth. We had vegetables only once a week,' he recalls the experience of those days. In course of time some leprosy patients were also part of the household and Tai took up sole responsibility of cooking and cleaning. But Tai had started developing some serious health problems, and in addition she became pregnant with her second child.

During her second pregnancy, Tai unfortunately contracted typhoid and took to bed. The burden of all the household work fell on Baba's shoulders: cooking, cleaning and taking care of the baby son Vikas. The tasks were too many, given the fact that Baba was already preoccupied with the leprosy training and treatment work. Therefore, for a short period Vikas had to be placed in the local maternity home.

A second son – Prakash – was born to the Amtes in December 1948. Tai's health was at a low ebb all this while, and as if enough was not enough, she developed a painful abscess, before the baby was a year old. Baba was at the end of his tether but instead of cowering under his difficulties he chose to tower over them by taking the best decision that was in sight. He migrated with his family to Dattapur, so that in addition to attending to his own family he could pursue his service to the cause of leprosy comfortably. Here, the Amtes stayed in one room on the maternity hospital grounds. But happy days were yet far. Tai continued to be sick, this time with a low fever, which persisted despite treatment. Tuberculosis was suspected and detected. Consequently she was asked to vacate the hospital quarters for fear that she might pass on the infection to others, especially to the president of the organization, whose room happened to be adjacent to the one occupied by the Amtes.

These were testing times and Baba was not one to relent or recoil. He was made of sterner stuff. He showed this by erecting a tent in the compound of another maternity home, which was under construction and stayed there for the next two months, with his sick wife and infant sons.

Yet even in the midst of such ordeals, Baba continued planning for a programme of welfare work for the benefit of leprosy-afflicted people. He enthused his friends to join him in founding an organization, the Maharogi Sewa Samiti (MSS), dedicated to the rehabilitation of the leprosy patients. In course of time, statutory requirements for its registration were completed. The MSS was established in 1949, with the main aim of treatment and rehabilitation of leprosy patients.

During this time Baba had one last cataclysmic confrontation with his father as a result of which he gave up all his rights and title to the ancestral property. Prior to this he had given up his law practice. Truly a pauper in the financial sense, he however now possessed a precious commodity – an all-consuming desire to mitigate the misery of the leprosy-stricken.

By now, Baba had completed his basic education in treatment of the dreaded disease, so he decided to go to the Tropical School of Medicine at Calcutta, for a systematic study of leprosy and attending their short term diploma course. However, admission to the course was open only to medical graduates. It is reported that Pundit Jawaharlal Nehru intervened on his behalf and he subsequently got admission. The well-known research scholar and leprosy expert Dr. Dharmendra was the director of that institution.

The problem of monitoring the growth of leprosy germs under laboratory conditions, outside the body of leprosy patients, has bothered the medical scientists interested in the treatment and prevention of leprosy. Dr. Armauer Hansen had identified Mycobacterium leprae the leprosy causing microbe, about 125 years ago. But during this interval, scientists had not succeeded in growing these microbes artificially in a culture. Barring very few exceptions, no living beings except humans are afflicted by the disease. Therefore, the microbes could not be injected into the bodies of other animals to help prepare its vaccine.

An interesting incident occurred at the Tropical School of Medicine while Baba was undergoing training of leprosy treatment there. During the training, Dr. Dharmendra mentioned that since all experiments to inject leprosy germs into other living creatures to find a cure for the disease had failed, the only option was to try injecting a human being with the germs and help develop a vaccine. Even though this was suggested in jest, Baba took it in all seriousness. He offered himself as a guinea pig to have the leprosy bacilli injected into his body. Though his teachers did not approve of this idea, Baba persisted. 'There were two tests to which he subjected himself: the injection of dead bacilli and subsequently the injection of live bacilli. Fortunately, the tests did not have any effect on him. Before taking the tests, he had taken Indu's permission to go ahead with them. Baba says, 'About this experiment I had no fear. If I contracted the disease, I had the assurance that Indu would take care of me. Such a strong assurance arising out of a close and understanding relationship provides an emotional security, which even the most reputed insurance company is ill-equipped to give and enables human beings to sail fearlessly through the storms of life.' When Tai says, 'Our life has been a continuous hurdles race and endurance test,' it is easy to perceive that it was their being one at heart that generated fortitude in them to face their hurdles headlong.

Though without previous medical training, Baba, who had been refused permission to study medicine by his parents, completed the training first among 28 postgraduate medics. By the time he returned home, the treatment of leprosy had been revolutionized by the discovery and availability of diamino diphenyl sulphone, making leprosy curable. But the effect of the drug on a patient was far from immediate and the danger of highly infectious patients passing on the disease to others still remained.

With this wonder drug in hand, he began treating leprosy patients in 60 villages around Warora. Baba discovered that leprosy is the least infectious of all communicable diseases. It was infectious only in its earlier stages and, if discovered early, could be stopped from numbing nerve endings which lead to disfiguring of affected body parts. Another discovery he made was that more serious than the disease itself was the stigma attached to it. In those times and in areas as remote as Warora, lepers were shunned by society. Leprosy was an accursed disease that had no cure. What he found much more serious was what he terms today 'the leprosy of the mind'. Baba's mission was to fight that prejudice.

The citizens of Warora shuddered at the vagaries of this mad lawyer. His involvement with Harijans and latrine cleaners was just about tolerable. But they could not bring themselves to support his enthusiasm for this hideous disease. He was socially ostracized.

Undeterred by this, the Amte couple would move across villages on foot with some of their cured patients and sit quietly at the weekly bazaar. Spotting them, other leprosy affected people would muster the courage to approach them and so the community grew – in uncanny silent communication between those condemned to silence by an intolerant and ignorant social system. Young Vikas contributed his mite, keeping the home fires burning, while his parents moved from village to village, offering cure and spreading awareness about leprosy.

In 1951, Baba applied to the state government for land to set up a new kind of leprosarium, which would not be restricted to mere provision of refuge and treatment, but would rebuild the spirit and dignity of those shattered by social revulsion, scorn and ostracism.

That year Baba obtained from the Madhya Pradesh Government, for the activities of the MSS, 50 acres of barren and rock-ridden wasteland, covered with scrub and trees. This land, 5km from Warora town and located near the Chandrapur–Nagpur road, was part of a disused quarry and was the habitat of tigers, panthers, bears, wild boars, snakes and scorpions. The nearest well was 2km away! Today Baba recalls, 'Perhaps it was symptomatic that there was nothing but a tangle of boulders, roots and creepers. Outcaste land, for outcaste people. This was our lot from now on.'

In 1951 MSS became a registered society and this completed Baba and Tai's first giant leap, chequered with pain and perseverance, in the direction of their destination. 'Amte's Miracle', as BBC economist Graham Turner described it in his book *More Than Conquerors*, was begun with half a dozen rupees, a lame cow and 50 acres of forest land in a stone quarrying area. With only the lepers, his wife and himself to do all the work from forest reclamation to leprosy treatment, it was a battle of survival at first.

The foundation to a gigantic endeavour had been laid but the tedious task of construction still lay ahead; the conversion of the wasteland into a wonderland. For this there was an inexhaustible resource: his dreams, his vision, his enterprise. With these in hand was born Anandwan, Amte's Garden of Joy, and Baba Amte himself.

'I found out that while physical leprosy is perfectly curable, mental leprosy is not. Our society has psychological anaesthesia. I have always been drawn to this fellowship of pain. I think He created pain, because without it there would be no tenderness. It is very easy for a man to love God, but it is difficult for him to follow the commandment – love thy neighbour. I have been called a miracle man, but it is not I who wrought the miracle, it is they, the inmates of Anandwan. A claw snatched colours from the rainbow and created wonders on the earth. The herd doesn't wait for the wounded deer. Therefore, someone else must help,' said Baba Amte.

CHAPTER 6

Anandwan – From Wasteland to Wonderland

I sought my soul,
My soul I could not see,
I sought my God,
My God eluded me,
I sought my brother,
And I found all three.

(Words of an anonymous poet,
inscribed on the walls at Anandwan)

Murlidhar Devidas Amte, at the age of 36, moved on to the all-rock, no-water, godforsaken wilderness of 50 acres, which he chose to call Anandwan – or the Garden of Joy! Along with him came too his wife, their young sons – Vikas and Prakash – and six leprosy patients from the Dattapur leprosy clinic. They also brought with them a lame cow, four dogs for protection against the wild animals, four shovels, three pickaxes, two hoes, two cross-bars, five axes, bedding, cooking utensils and Rs. 14.

Before permanent shelters could be built, the four dogs were taken, one by one, and eaten by the panthers. Tai recalls that the panthers took the dogs from under the beds while they slept. On one occasion Baba was bitten by a panther and on another, he took off his shirt to find that scorpions were using it as a passage to the ground. The worst problem was with the rats. The rats would eat the insensitive limbs of the leprosy patients when they slept. It was a while before the rats could be got rid off. Not only wild animals made life miserable for the Amtes, but in those early days, even friends would not have tea with them and their children had no one to play with. Baba recalls, more in amusement than in anger, that a leprosy worker in a remote place was more isolated than a leprosy patient. But his response to such a situation is a classic case of turning the pessimism of the mind into an optimism of the will.

To turn the scrubland into a habitable place, Herculean efforts were needed. The jungle had to be cleared, wild animals driven away, scrub and bushes uprooted and burnt and the land tilled and prepared for agriculture. But more than anything else, water scarcity posed the major problem. A well was the greatest necessity. So Baba and his army of six lepers set upon digging a well in earnest. This is what Baba says of the experience: 'After almost six weeks, when we were about 34 feet down, the rock was becoming a little moist. It was May; the temperature was 47 degree celsius in the shade. Inside the hole it was fearfully hot. Then a bee followed by a butterfly came to the moisture. Two days later when we arrived in the morning, we found a frog happily sitting in a puddle of water in the stones. We worshipped the water with white flowers and milk. Then the rest of the day we sat by our well, just staring delightedly at the water.' 'More sweat has gone into the wells we dug than the water found in them,' Baba puts it poetically.

A shelter without walls was the first home of the pioneering group of the community which came to be called Anandwan. Another hut was built a few days later. Tai says, 'Before this second hut was built, both of us used to walk 2/3 miles daily, with a tiffin carrier and water container in hand, making the children walk for some distance and carrying them for the rest till we reached the Anandwan forest. We could not even afford a pedal cycle. Before the first hut was constructed, the leprosy patients who had arrived from Dattapur, stayed with us. I cooked for them all. Both of us attended to such chores as cleaning the pots, washing clothes, drawing several bucketfuls of water from the well, preparing hand-pound rice, wheat dough and grinding grams. A couple of Scheduled Caste students were also staying with us.'

On 21st June 1951, the settlement was inaugurated by Acharya Vinoba Bhave, who thus described it: 'Its name Anandwan is most appropriate.... This is not a lepers' colony, not a home or settlement for leprosy patients. Here a new epic of service and labour is being written.'

More patients began arriving at Anandwan. Medical services for leprosy patients were started with Baba as the qualified health worker in charge, besides acting as wood-cutter, well-digger and farmer. Tai ran the catering department. Two cows, which were originally brought from a Gorakshan Shala to provide company for the patients, were the predecessors of the cows and buffaloes which came later to make the dairy. Seeing the udders of the cows being chock-full, Tai, who had no experience in milking them, set to do the task by tying the hind limbs. 'I got kicks from the cows. My palms got swollen and every nerve in my arm ached severely.... Many people came to Anandwan to verify that the milking was not done by leprosy-affected hands (because the milk sent to the market was often rejected as being touched by leprosy patients).'

Within two years Anandwan became self-sufficient in everything. By the end of 1954 there were 60 patients and six wells. The land, having been made cultivable, was yielding vegetables and grains in very large quantities. After the requirements of the inmates of Anandwan were met, the surplus was supplied to the nearby markets. Despite the fact that the quality of the produce from Anandwan was far superior to that of produce from other places, people desisted from buying it, fearing that it might have been infected by the patients. Yet gradually, lured by lower prices and better quality, a few people gathered courage to purchase them and later others followed suit.

Baba says that he has lots of friends. His friends are an odd mixture of Indians and foreigners. Pierre Opplinger was a Swiss social worker, who became one of Baba's and Anandwan's dearest friends. Pierre belonged to Service Civil International, a Swiss organization which helped welfare schemes the world over through the gift of manual labour. In 1954, this organization had been working at the Gandhi Ashram at Sewagram, 60 miles away. Baba heard about them and invited them to visit Anandwan. Led by Pierre Opplinger, a team of 50 volunteers, representing 14 nations and 23 languages, came to Anandwan and undertook a construction programme lasting four months. In four months they put up six buildings, including a clinic and two hospital wards. The presence of these volunteers at Anandwan helped dispel the myths that the locals had spread about leprosy. Until the arrival of the volunteers, the people of Warora had viewed Baba's project with skepticism, fear and resentment. There was widespread fear of leprosy, coupled with the misconception that the disease was a result of the afflicted having committed some serious sin, either in this or a previous life, and were suffering punishment at the hands of God. But the presence of the volunteers instilled courage and confidence in the local youth, who began trickling in to render their services at Anandwan.

Realizing that organization of the leprosy-afflicted was not the solution to the problem, Baba improvised an intelligent plan to tackle the situation. As early as 1957, he started a survey of the villages around Warora for the early detection and treatment of leprosy patients. Through his 'trace and treat' campaign he discovered new patients, whom he began treating in his weekly clinics. In 1957, he had started 11 clinics in a radius of 30 miles, each of which he visited weekly. Baba cleverly used this campaign to eradicate the myths and unfounded fears wound around the disease by talking effectively to the people he encountered.

It was at around this time that Mother Gavrilia, the Greek nun, visited Anandwan and was very impressed by the work being carried on there by Baba. She stayed there, initially for two months but came back several times in the five years that she spent in India, and began rendering medical aid to the patients. The deep bond formed between these two great souls lasted till Mother Gavrilia's death.

The more he worked with leprosy patients, the more Baba realized that even though their bodies had been brutally disfigured, nature had miraculously compensated them with spirits far stronger than those of their able-bodied brethren. The energy emanating from such charged spirits could not be left to bleed away. He decided to so develop their abilities that they would not have to depend on others. 'Work builds and charity destroys' was the motto he used in order to utilize the energy of those that had been cured of the disease. So at Anandwan everyone, the cured, the convalescing and the healthy, took part in all the work. According to their ability the inmates contributed to farming, dairy-farming, construction work, cleaning, cooking and a dozen other such activities. And in turn Baba became their physician.

Tai remembers that, in those days, her day started at 3 a.m. Baba's lunch had to be prepared and packed, to be carried with him when he set out every morning at 4 o'clock for the day's clinic located in one of the villages. Baba was a stickler for punctuality. If the food was late by a few minutes, he would be annoyed and would leave in a huff without the lunch packet. Tai would on those days renounce her lunch too. After his return from the clinic, Baba rendered medical services to the leprosy patients of Anandwan. Though he tried to, Baba could not get a regular doctor for the patients. A couple of doctors who did join the clinic for short periods were scared of getting infected and eventually left the place. Baba remembers one doctor who used to wash not only his hands but even his bicycle thoroughly with dettol after attending to the patients. In the absence of a qualified medical practitioner, Baba worked alone, giving injections, distributing drugs and dressing sores and ulcers. This carried on until 1974 when Baba's sons Vikas and Prakash both graduated from medical school and joined Anandwan as qualified doctors. Paul Brad, a renowned leprologist and orthopedic surgeon wrote to Vikas in 1981 expressing his amazement at and appreciation of Baba's ability in carrying on leprosy work without ever receiving any adequate help from doctors.

In 1954, Anandwan acquired a number of cows and set up what became a productive dairy. In 1956, the community took charge of its first vehicle – a jeep. Since the leprosy patients were forbidden to hold a driving license, Baba did most of the driving. Continuous driving over rough tracks is what eventually led to Baba's spinal disorder.

In 1957 oil lamps were replaced with electric lamps, with which Anandwan entered a new phase of development. The first industrial unit of Anandwan was the tin-can workshop which came into being due to the efforts of the then Indian Ambassador to Switzerland Mr. Velodi. Once as Mrs. Velodi was moving through Bern city, she saw on a building a board 'Swiss Ousland IIF' (Swiss Aid Abroad). Out of curiosity she collected information about the institution, which happened to be a conduit for giving aid to different parts of the world institutions working for social causes. Since Mr. and Mrs. Velodi were aware of Baba's work at Anandwan, they recommended Anandwan to Ousland IIF for grant of aid. Once again Pierre Opplinger, who was heading the organization, was instrumental in sanctioning the grant. The money came as a response from the French-speaking districts of Switzerland, following the appeal of Swiss Aid Abroad. By giving up a meal and contributing the cost of the meal to the project, the people generated the amount on behalf of Anandwan. On 28th November 1960, the Tin Can Project was formally inaugurated by Mr. Cuta, the Swiss Ambassador to India at that time.

The Tin Can Project manufactured articles of common use like tiffin carriers, lanterns, strainers, etc. Along with grains and vegetables grown at Anandwan, these articles of daily use were sent for sale to the local market.

A primary school was opened next in 1961 called 'Gokul'. In 1962, Anandwan's post office started functioning. In 1966, a school for the blind came up with aid from the Netherlands.

Anandwan was able to raise enough funds by the sale of their products, so Baba's next plan was to open two colleges, the builders of which were to be the leprosy-afflicted inmates of Anandwan. One of Baba's friends recalls how Baba called him and others on a day in October 1963 to a spot on the grounds of Anandwan and unfolded his plan dramatically. A group of cured people stood there, ready with pickaxes, to begin digging. Baba announced that the construction work for the college building was about to commence and everything would be ready on time for the first batch of students to be admitted for the academic year 1964-65. Even though some of his friends thought that Baba was straying from his chosen mission of serving the leprosy patients and that higher education was unconnected with his commitments, Baba stood by his plan, as he had geared it to solid purposes. Warora did not have a college and a college would fulfil the desire of the rural boys and girls who aspired for a higher education. Baba hoped that the young people graduating from the college would help others in shedding their prejudices against leprosy and its patients. But the main objective behind opening these colleges by involving the patients in the construction work, however, was that the leprosy-affected would be at the giving end instead of always being at the receiving end. The journey from medical cure to empowerment would result in the scorned and rejected giving back to the social mainstream many times more than what they had ever asked for.

The journey had, however, taken a heavy toll on its first soldier. In 1964, Baba was told by his doctors that the agonizing pain in his back was the result of a progressive degeneration of the spine, which they diagnosed as severe cervical spondylosis. After spending a few years on medication, his friends collected enough money to send him to Wimbledon (U.K.), for a major operation of the spine. The operation was performed resulting in the removal of a few of his lower vertebrae and a replacement of two by animal bone. Baba mocked his condition thus: 'I'm a spineless man now.'

Due to Baba's firm resolve, the Anandwan College of Arts, Science and Commerce was a reality for all to witness by July 1964. As expected at first there were all kinds of rumours adrift about the college, that the college was only for the leprosy-stricken and their children and that some faculty members themselves were suffering from the disease. The first principal and a faculty member together toured the entire district to quell these rumours and later when Baba's sons joined the college, all misunderstandings subsided. In 1965 the Anandwan College of Agriculture also came into being.

To begin with, marriages were disallowed at Anandwan but later realizing the loneliness and desire of companionship amongst the patients, Baba accepted the idea of marriage. In a simple ceremony eight pairs were married in the first batch. Since the buildings constructed till then were designed to accommodate only single occupants, a new unit called 'Mukti-Sadan' was constructed to settle in the married couples. This unit was inaugurated on 17th November 1962 by the great social reformer Sant Tukodji.

Anandwan was growing by leaps and bounds and the world around stood back to watch in amazement. Baba's seemingly impossible dream was turning into reality. But Baba had envisioned not only a physically comfortable but also a creatively contented lifestyle for those shunned by society. For this he started a three-day programme called 'Mitra Melawa' (a get-together of friends). This was a cultural festival to which the public in general was invited. Artists like musicians, singers and dramatists were invited from outside to perform and entertain the residents of Anandwan. Encouraged and inspired by these performances, the ones with inherent talents at Anandwan too began staging dramas and singing at these festivals. On one such occasion, Mr. P.L. Deshpande, a renowned writer, got interested in Baba's work. During his first visit to Anandwan, he happened to see the leprosy patients rehearsing a drama for the 'Mitra Melawa'. Mr. Deshpande mused, 'Usually people avoid seeing leprosy patients. Here Baba is putting them on the stage for all to see.' He found the whole idea very fascinating. The play that the patients were rehearsing was from the Hindu Puranas, a story of Lord Krishna, where Krishna had to be portrayed rotating the *Sudarshana Chakra* on his finger. But unfortunately the patient in the role of Krishna had no fingers. The problem was solved by substituting a wooden finger for the fingerless one. Mr. Deshpande was fascinated by the all-round development of people at Anandwan, whom society had discarded because of a prejudice, but in whose abilities Baba believed. Like others Mr. Deshpande was bowled over by Baba's sacrifice and service of the sick and secluded. The outcome was that he gave a generous donation for the construction of an auditorium, with a stage and also an open-air stage for the staging of cultural programmes. The auditorium was completed in 1976 and called 'Muktangan'.

On Mr. Deshpande's advice, ceremonious tree plantation was also introduced as part of 'Mitra Melawa'. The practice was adapted from Tagore's Shantiniketan. It is the simple activity of planting saplings in an atmosphere of jubilation and expectation. The sapling to be planted is taken in all splendour inside an ornately decorated palanquin carried in a procession. The sapling is then ceremoniously planted to the accompaniment of the song: 'Oh! young sapling, you are our guest today,' sung by the Anandwanians.

On one occasion, during the 'Mitra Melawa', the chief guest put eloquently in words the reasons due to which people, including renowned artists, came in hordes to attend the festival:

> We come here to bring out our innermost honesty and integrity. I and you alike become honest and open. This is a place which does not allow you to put on airs or appearances. I wonder whether we can call this a tourist centre. In a sense, the world at large is a tourist centre. We come from somewhere, stay for a while and proceed to some unknown destination. We specially visit the Ajanta-Ellora caves to see the ruins there but a disfigured person does not attract us in the same way as a disfigured monument. Baba the poet, who has helped us see this hidden beauty, is in our midst here. Do come to Anandwan as tourists but you will find that this tour has brought a basic change in you.
>
> Here no inducements or invitations are given to anybody. No travelling expenses and honorarium are paid. Why do people then come here even cancelling commitments made earlier? What is the secret? Eminent musicians and vocalists feel proud to entertain the sufferers

> here, not for any recognition but merely to create some happy moments in the life of the unfortunate residents… here the language is that of love.… I honestly believe that pain reveals more truths than the scriptures. Anandwan has been organized by a poet. Baba has expressed his poetry through words as well as deeds. Anandwan symbolizes Baba's 'living poem', which you can see with your own eyes.
>
> The cleanliness here is not on account of your expected arrival. This is a permanent feature of this place. No cleaning drive is undertaken here in honour of someone's visit. You may come here at any time, with or without pre-intimation and find Anandwan equally clean and beautiful.
>
> We have seen here the will to live. The leprosy patients themselves looked after us. The food we ate was grown by these hands. It therefore was not a mere means of satisfying one's hunger but a spiritually enriched offering.... When people ask you on return what you found there, do tell them that you found yourself.

Even though Baba's condition of spondylosis and later the operation confined him to bed, he did not lose a single moment there too. His mind was journeying in the world of ideas though his body was laid up in bed. His sickbed, which he thought would become a coffin, became instead, 'a womb for the conception and birth of new ideas'. The man who had overcome his primordial fears was not going to be done in so easily. The spirit of the man that inspired so many to overcome their physical disabilities fought back with renewed vigour. His body did less but his mind went flying in search of newer horizons. By 1971, Baba's elder son Vikas had graduated from medical school and joined the Anandwan hospital. He had passed his MBBS degree from Nagpur and completed a specialization course in leprosy treatment. A year later Dr. Bharti, Vikas's wife, also joined the hospital. Vikas and Bharti not only began looking after the hospital but were supervising other activities at Anandwan as well. And Baba, after having converted a scrubland of 50 acres into a heaven of 450 acres and entrusting it to the hands of his son and daughter-in-law, began planning another project.

CHAPTER 7

Anandwan – Its Units, Activities and Foreign Funding

> At Anandwan, human beings who happen to be leprosy patients and those usually considered 'disabled' like the blind and the deaf, enter the development process as responsible 'subjects' – those who know and act, in contrast to 'objects' which are known and acted upon. Nothing but awakening of consciousness can explain the marvels typical of the place: structures, strong and functional, built without architects, engineers and contractors, weavers without fingers, leprosy patients successfully insisting on being licensed to drive heavy duty trucks; a man who cannot walk managing the industrial training centre moving on a tricycle fabricated with in-house talent and materials; a person without previous experience in printing, running a press with competence; a one-handed cashier who makes up for a slight slowness by unusual thoroughness; a master tailor who cannot use his hands freely, training tailors from neighbouring villages....
>
> (From a report published on Anandwan by UNICEF, New Delhi)

By early 1960s Anandwan housed 600 patients, while Baba took care of an additional 4000 in local clinics. Only serious patients were confined to hospital beds. The rest participated wholeheartedly in a diverse variety of activities including modern agriculture and industrial units. Undoubtedly, it is to Baba's credit that he visualized, managed and paved the way for the stupendous growth of this project. But it was the sheer grit and sweat of the leprosy patients that was instrumental in transforming the barren, rocky stretch into a productive green land. Anandwan became a living experiment in rural development and community living. Its achievement was self-sufficiency in a way that was not exploitative of either people or non-human nature. Outside agencies began to come regularly and study this unique experiment that kept succeeding and exceeding everybody's expectations. The MSS was travelling on a long journey. Starting with a concern for individual development through treatment, rehabilitation and active inducement of leprosy patients in communes shunned by the rest of the community, the Samiti moved on to the assimilation of the handicapped in the same commune.

Since almost all members of the commune were either leprosy patients or the physically handicapped, appropriate tools and technology were developed to provide work to all members, irrespective of their handicap. As a result of this, nearly all articles, with the exception of only salt, sugar and oil, were being manufactured within the precincts of the community by those that had stumpy fingers but sublime spirits. 'There are no lepers here,' says Baba, 'only carpenters, masons, farmers....'

Baba was often impatient, dismissive, even angry, but always self-correcting. However, everyone realized that his anger was the anger of love. His commitment was so final that he got impatient with others who did not have his determination. Although Baba was a strict disciplinarian to the inhabitants regarding institutional matters, they acknowledge that this attitude made them cohesive as a unit and productive to their utmost capacity. Anandwan began with two huts but later as more and more people started coming in, Baba sought assistance from Service Civil International, for construction work. But after this endeavour by outsiders, the engineers, labourers and masons from among the inhabitants provided manpower to construct other buildings. Sukh-Sadan was constructed in 1968. The idea was that each married couple would take in an aged patient, treating him/her as a parent. During the day as the young couple was engaged in contributing to the various activities carried out at Anandwan, the aged 'parent', would look after the children. Laudable as the idea was, it did not succeed in reality. So, ultimately the 'aged parent' was excluded from the family and housed elsewhere. The aged patients of Sneh-Savli (the shade of affection), who are of the pre-sulphone era and are severely deformed, stay at this unit.

In 1979, Swiss Aid gave a grant for the construction of ex unit called Krishi-Niketan, which was completed in 1981. It houses both married as well as single patients. It has a common kitchen, a godown, a dispensary, a bullock shed and a garage. The inhabitants living here participate in the agricultural practices of the community. Udhyog-Bhavan houses only single men and women. It has a kitchen, a godown, a dining hall and an open space for entertainment.

Baba's work with the leprosy-affected soon began to diversify into other areas such as hostels for the blind, deaf, mute and the orthopaedically disabled. The opening of the vocational training facilities for the blind, deaf, mute and orthopaedically handicapped necessitated the provision of hostel facilities. There were also dormitories for the leprosy-affected children.

In 1979, Baba opened a home called Uttarayan for the senior citizens, whom he visualized as a sort of wisdom bank for the institution, contributing from their rich experiences and at the same time adding years to their life.

Gokul, the orphanage, has an interesting origin. An infant girl found abandoned at the Warora railway station was brought to Anandwan and Baba and Tai were requested to keep the child. This gave them the idea of having a home for the non-leprosy affected children of the leprosy-affected. This led to the establishment of Gokul in 1983, through the efforts of hundreds of school children of Maharashtra, who collected a sum of Rs. 3,50,000 in response to the appeal by the Amtes. The children here have formed a deep bond with Tai, as she takes a personal interest in their upbringing.

Baba acquired a new foreign friend in the person of Count Tarnowsky, a Pole by birth, who had migrated to England during the Second World War. Tarnowsky was a polio-disabled person and confined to a wheel chair. However, his confinement did not deter him from travelling the world over on a mission to see for himself the services provided for the physically disabled in different parts of the world. In 1968, he happened to visit Anandwan and felt drawn to the kindred spirit of Baba. He writes, 'I cannot resist the enthusiasm of others, and I don't expect others to resist my enthusiasm.'

Tarnowsky's enthusiasm for contributing physically and financially to better the plight of the disabled merged with Baba's enthusiasm for the same cause. The happy result of this amalgamation was the drawing up of a plan for the opening of 'The House of Opportunities' called 'Sandhi Niketan'. It was planned to be a training workshop for the rehabilitation of the disabled. The Count donated a generous amount towards the construction of the building, for which work commenced on 1st February 1970. Besides donating money, the Count was not far behind in contributing manually during the construction work. Sitting in his wheelchair and moving within the restricted mobility, he worked with the residents of Anandwan with their, 'telltale marks of leprosy disfigurement', whom he accepted without any reservations. The joy of participating in a humanitarian enterprise was so great that it transcended the oppressive summer heat, which had turned his 'wheelchair into a hot oven'. The building was ready for house blessing on 21st April 1970. Sandhi Niketan, today is the apex body for the industrial activities of the MSS. It trains the handicapped in handcrafts, carpentry, leather-work, tailoring, spinning and weaving, wood-carving, cane work and making of greeting cards.

In addition to the aforementioned residential units there are over a dozen productive or industrial ventures at Anandwan, which are run by its inmates and which multiply not only finances but add to their dignity as well. The first of these industrial units to be initiated, of course, was the tin can project in 1960. After this followed numerous other ventures over the years like printing section, weaving section, handloom section, power-loom section, leather-craft section, pottery section, electric and plumbing, carpentry and tailoring sections. The tailoring section trains mostly women to become seamstresses, who stitch clothes for the inmates as well as for customers. It is rumoured that the famous Bollywood actor Nana Patekar too gets a few outfits designed here!

THE ARTIST IS NOT A SPECIAL KIND OF MAN BUT EVERY MAN IS A SPECIAL KIND OF ARTIST

This is the axiom that stands bold and clear at the entrance of the Art section. And once you enter, the truth of it strikes you full face: cards, driftwood, dried leaves, stones, wax, empty bottles, matchsticks and matchboxes, worn-out tyres, thrown-away pieces of cloth and broken bangles, everything that nature has provided and man has left to decay, has been moulded into exquisite pieces by the discarded, disowned people here, and every creation contributes towards keeping the economy ticking.

Further on is one of the other important units – the plastic reuse unit. Anandwan has a full-fledged hospital that also generates medical waste. Recycling this waste reduces the impact on the environment. Saline bottles become Christmas trees, with little ornaments hanging from them. Intricate works of art are created from empty sachets. These sachets with high-gloss and four-colour printing, lend themselves to colourful decorative pieces. Elsewhere in the world these sachets only add to the rubbish in the landfills. But at Anandwan they use them as raw materials for art! Residents also travel to nearby villages to collect plastic bags and other reusable trash. Then they wash, sanitize and sort it. Thereafter, they are shredded to a cotton-like consistency to fill into mattresses and pillows. The ingenuity is fascinating and inspiring.

At Anandwan everyone has a role to play. There are carpenters, barbers, cobblers, cooks, students, architects, doctors, engineers, psychologists... and all of them are part of an exquisite productive collage. Office administrators, weavers, a man on his way to work, carpet artisans, metal works employees... all Anandwan residents contribute to its economy in some way or the other. It doesn't matter what the work is: it is an important part of the economic fabric. When one has free time, one is encouraged to plant seedlings, so that one is always engaged and active. The older residents monitor the younger children and teach them values. *This* is the face of productivity at Anandwan.

In order to keep this giant industrial dragon well-oiled, the CSA or the Centre for Social Action was organized. The goal of the CSA is to have dialogue amongst the concerned planners, administrators, technologists, social workers and social scientists. The centre seeks to understand the complexities of the problems of poverty and economic development from the perspective of social justice and develop a vision for a new type of society where social development and social justice will move together, hand in hand. The CSA is geared towards developing an alternative strategy of development, which covers:

1. Biomass farming: This concerns the production of fuels, fodder, fibres and construction materials. Agriculture and tree planting have to be carefully integrated from considerations of ecology and income production.
2. Development of efficient methods of irrigation.
3. Conservation of non-renewable resources of energy and development of renewable sources of energy.
4. Efficient management of land and water.
5. Utilization of organic fertilizers and less dependence on chemicals.

These ideas are not mere words on paper as government ventures. They have been put to test by undertaking such projects as:

1. Agro-forestry project in which local trees which grow fast, are used for fuel, fodder and timber, and become fertilizers, have been planted on many hectares of poor land.
2. Pasture development: Some hectares of land which were devoted to growing cattle fodder under this project are a happy grazing ground for the cattle of Anandwan today.

3. Multi-tier silvi-pasture system: In a section of the agro-forestry area, shade-tolerant grasses have been grown on the ground and climbers in the middle tier, to optimize the productivity of the land.

They eat the food they produce
They weave the cloth they wear
They live in the houses they construct.
They are the most complete human beings!

The medical activities began at Anandwan under a wall-less, thatched hut that served as an indoor clinic, with Baba serving as doctor. Soon realizing that this was insufficient, Baba walked for miles in the neighbouring areas providing cure and spreading awareness about the disease. In 1971, when Vikas, Baba and Tai's older son, graduated from medical college at Nagpur and joined the indoor clinic at Anandwan, he gave a new impetus to the medical facilities provided by the MSS. Today the 'Shirdi Sai Baba Hospital' at Anandwan has a well-manned laboratory, an operation theatre, a team of well-trained doctors and nursing staff, and a unit for making special shoes. Volunteers, in the form of doctors and nurses from many a foreign land, consider themselves privileged to participate in the service of the old, the frail and the sick. I met a nurse, a member of Dr. Albert Schweitzer's Foundation, the 'Nouvelle Planet', bent with the burden of her 70 years, who had travelled half the world from Switzerland, to diligently devote three hours of her time in the morning and one hour of it in the evening in the hospital! Baba began his work with the purpose of helping the leprosy-affected to snatch back their rightful dignity that society had stripped them of, by showing them how their deformed bodies were capable of as harsh a physical labour as that of any able-bodied man, in order for them to earn their livelihood. He, however, realized very soon the importance of arming these people with another weapon – education.

The first instrument that was to provide this weapon was in

the form of a primary school started in 1961. It had four grades and the syllabus followed was that set by the local education authority. Gokul, The Child Haven, was to be the residential facility of this school. the school was for the children of the leprosy patients within or outside the community. On the trail of this school followed another school, Prakasachi Sala, School of Light, in 1966 for the visually impaired, with aid from the Netherlands. The school has a Braille library and a Braille typewriter.

Anandwan College of Arts, Sciences and Commerce was opened in 1964 amidst the apprehensions of not only Baba's adversaries, but also friends and well-wishers. Even more surprising was the fact that the leprosy-eaten hands had built and furnished it, cementing brick by brick to raise the structure and nailing plank by plank to create the chairs and tables! Next to be erected was the Anand-Niketan College of Agriculture in 1968, by those very hands that had melted like candlesticks, but resurrected faiths that were ever leaping up like the candle flames. Today these colleges not only empower the residents of Anandwan and their children, but also accomodate all those who want to study there.

The hands that had repaid more than the debt that they owed to society belonged to those whose dreams had died. Baba not only dreamt their dreams, but also showed them the way to make them a reality.

Having been reared in a 'brotherhood of pain', in Baba's words, the Anandwanians have formed so strong a bond of selfless love, sacrifice and dedication towards each other that it would put to shame all relationships that pride themselves to be formed by ties of blood. In the era of communal living that begins with intolerance and is destined to end in destruction and unhappiness, they follow the simple yet happier way of community living. Living in these communities of theirs, one finds there are only happy people and honest people, who live with just one knowledge, that they have the strength to achieve anything through the power of sweat and trust in their innate abilities. Everybody works in this system. The relative quietness of the campus is striking – nobody raises his voice, quarrels, idles or argues here. The system works because it is highly decentralized and divided into teams. Everybody knows what is expected of him or her. The ideology practised here transcends all divisions of caste, community, religion, gender, sick and healthy persons. One does not see any ritual expressions of religion, no temples, no shrines in or near the premises. Everybody eats together. Food is served by women. Nobody asks for dishes that are not on the menu of the day. Everybody washes his or her own dish. Nobody, who knocks on the door of Anandwan is ever refused food and shelter. Guests are readily invited to stay overnight. Beds, bedsheets and mosquito nets are provided. They are neat, clean but spartan. It is hard to believe the existence of this happy world in the midst of a depraved one. Yet it is a reality.

The lively chitter-chatter of the women manning the community kitchens is comforting, assuring homeliness and inviting. The sight is even better. Women doubly wronged – one on account of merely being women, and in addition, inflicted with a dreaded disease – move proudly around in their domain, engaged in various activities – peeling, pounding, stirring *dals* (lentil soups) with large wooden ladles in large pots, sweeping, etc. They briefly look up to give shy smiles and nods to visitors by way of salutations and then return to their duties and the lively chitter-chatter once more. If you are lucky to visit the kitchen on a day when a special meal is being cooked for a special occasion or festival, you will be made to taste the 'special' on the menu. Each unit has one or more of these kinds of kitchens, their number depending on the number of inmates residing in that particular unit. While the rest of the residents of a unit are busy in either tilling, sowing, reaping, creating works of art, weaving, working at the tin factory or tending to the cows, the women in the kitchens prepare for them their hard-earned and hence rightly deserved meals. But more than all this, it is the camaraderie of these people that astounds you.

The term 'social worker' is inadequate to express the essence of Baba's work. The only word that could have done it is 'Baba'

– the father – who bandaged the bleeding wounds of the sick, educated them, taught them the value of labour, redefined dignity for them and not only that, also taught them to indulge in pleasure gratification once in a while through music, dance, drama and celebrations of all religious functions.

'All work and no play', this was the story of Jack but the people of Anandwan have a different tale. They are provided avenues to express themselves through any form of art that they choose. A variety of cultural activities are indulged in, through which is provided an opportunity to the cured and the convalescents to participate in life, and experience it in its holistic sense.

In a world which discarded them as waste, it was natural for these people to turn to God. And in order to praise his benevolence, for giving them a home as loving as Anandwan and a father as exalted as Baba, the best way was to sing His praises. Hence, singing of bhajans (hymns) – the easiest and most infectious form of singing – became an important form of recreation and an integral aspect of the cultural life at Anandwan. Bhajans have now become a means of relaxation and socializing. They form an enjoyable routine on Thursdays and Saturdays. Dramas were being performed at Anandwan even before the construction of the open-air theatre there called 'Muktangan'. In 1962, after the Chinese aggression, the patients had staged a drama and raised Rs 2000, which was donated to the national relief fund. In 1974, with a donation of rupees one lakh, 'Muktangan' was turned into an auditorium. This auditorium comes alive with the performance of the Anandwan orchestra, which comprises such artists as those whose limbs have been reduced to stumps, eyes into pools of perennial darkness and ears into numb appendages. Yet their music is pure honey to the able-bodied. Serene faces with such melodious voices reverberate in the silence of the enraptured audience which is made to see beyond the defects of the body of these performers and lose itself in the beats that emanate from the depths of the heart.

For those who cannot sing but appreciate music, the radio

and television sets provided at the units fulfil their need for entertainment. As the sun is rolling up its last rays and gearing to set, donned in an orange mantle with the feathered race in its trail, the lot at Anandwan, washed, combed and supped, is ready for some TV time. They assemble at a vantage point with a large cemented ground surrounded by concrete benches and a 29 inch TV set installed in a square cavity in a wall. Daily soaps are the favourites, followed by the national news and Bollywood songs and movies.

Another important aspect of the community living is celebration of religious festivals. Many of the religious festivals of India are socio-cultural festivals knitting the community by a tighter weave. At Anandwan the same spirit prevails. Major festivals of all religions are celebrated and they become delightful excuses for people to interact and understand each other.

Could the people the world over then sit back and not participate in the progress of the spectacle that was called Anandwan? No, they could not. So they reached out in whatever way – material as well as physical – and joined this honest endeavour of rehabilitation of the sick and the downtrodden. In addition to a hundred national, big and small, public and private ventures, a number of international organizations too are involved in sending out aid to the MSS:

1. The Service Civil International (SCI), a post World War I peace group, founded in 1920, was the first to provide financial and voluntary aid to Anandwan. In 1953, Alfred Knaus, a German and a member of this team, became the first foreigner to set foot on Anandwan soil. In 1990, SCI organized celebrations to mark the 70 years of its existence in Anandwan.
2. Count Tarnowski, founder of Take Heart Foundation of U.K. has been a close friend of Baba for the last 38 years. The first two chapters of his book, *The Unbeaten Track,* are devoted to Anandwan and all the proceeds from the sale of his book were donated to start 'Sandhi Niketan', the house

of opportunities. The Count has visited Anandwan 36 times in 38 years.

3. Swiss Aid Abroad has been the single largest donor to the MSS from 1960 to 1984. This agency has helped build several communes, hospitals, schools and colleges.
4. Since 1993, Nouvelle Planet, has organized several trips of European students to Anandwan. These students spend three weeks of their holidays working on various projects here. The Albert Schweitzer's Hospital Fund has also sent aid to Anandwan, via Nouvelle Planet.
5. In a unique children-to-children support programme, 'Kinder Postalzes' (Netherlands Committee of Children) organized to raise funds through walks, sales of stamps and other events for Anandwan's mentally and physically challenged children.
6. The renowned British economist Baroness Jackson of Lodsworth, Barbara Ward (first recipient of Nehru Award), donated her entire award money to the MSS.

More than half a century ago, the man who set out alone to realize a seemingly impossible vision was Murlidhar Devidas Amte. But gradually, with lepers as his only friends and his wife as his only supporter, he gave concrete shape to that vision, even as the world gaped in utter disbelief. He showed the world what the innate colossal strength of the spirit of man was capable of achieving, even though the mortal frame of the achievers had taken not only the beating of a dreaded disease, but more than that, the hatred of their fellow beings. He was acknowledged as the leader of those whom the world had disowned and as 'Baba', the father of humanity at large. He had proved his point.

After about four decades or more of relentless physical and moral effort, Baba left the whole enterprise that he had created with literally nothing but the sufferings of the disease-stricken, into the hands of his equally able, first-born Vikas. Having been bred in the realm of the pain of the forsaken, the broken and yet the brave, Vikas took to the only work he ever knew, with the dexterity of an expert. After completing his degree in medicine in 1971, Vikas initially served as a doctor at Anandwan. But gradually with Baba's deteriorating health and his increasing trust in the ability of his sons Vikas and Prakash, Baba left for them the legacy of carrying on the service of the needy. One by one Vikas shouldered responsibilities of various kinds, and today with Baba having been slowed down by a dozen ailments, Vikas is in complete charge as the Assistant Secretary and Medical Superintendent of the Maharogi Sewa Samiti. The World Health Organization has defined leprosy rehabilitation thus: 'By rehabilitation is meant the physical and mental restoration as far as possible, of all treated leprosy patients to normal activity, so that they may be able to assume a place in the home, society and industry.' Baba had realized the meaning of this axiom much before the WHO had put it into words, little wonder then that he was able to put it into action even when the world was merely reciting it to grasp its meaning. This was so because he had derived his meaning from the words of his hero, the Mahatma: 'Leprosy work is not mere relief, it is transforming frustration of life into the joy of dedication, personal ambition into selfless service.'

Says Baba, 'Anandwan provides rehabilitation of leprosy patients along with their treatment. All their lives have been strung together with the common thread of suffering and so they could show their mettle. Just as I have seen a healthy mind in sick bodies at Anandwan, I have seen sick and frustrated minds in healthy bodies in the outside world.... When Anandwan became self-reliant, the second chapter of my life's mission was completed. In world context, the history of leprosy patients achieved an epoch-making landmark. "The House of Charity" was converted into a battlefield of productivity.'

CHAPTER 8

Ashokwan and Somnath

Like Anandwan, Baba's other projects were also launched in difficult environments – unproductive and uninhabitable lands – discarded and forgotten by the people as well as the government. But Baba brought to life such barren tracts of land with the assistance of a portion of humanity, even more forgotten and discarded than these tracts of land – the leprosy-stricken. People who had given up all hope of life and just waited around to melt and rot away to death were so revived by Baba's charisma that they toiled and sweated on a dead patch of earth, giving it, in turn, the hope of life that Baba had given them. And these were the sublime words that Baba used as tools to infuse life into these degenerated souls, 'Do not mourn for what you lost and do not insult what you have: make the most of what you have.' He put 'sound minds' into 'unsound bodies' in order for them to regain their confidence and self-worth, which would help them to change the worst, the most irretrievable situations around them and get a hold on their own shattered lives.

Baba did not rest after his Anandwan project was completed but went ahead full steam. The strength of his own steam and a restless soul, kept him moving ahead into other barren lands and reaching other broken people, as and where he could find them so that he could revive as many of these as was possible for him to do. Hurt and saddened by the hypocrisy and indifference of the people towards the ill and needy, Baba was forever coming up with new ideas for providing relief to those in pain.

'Every day I am in search of myself. Sometimes I am isolated.

The wound is not visible though I am bruised. In such solitude, my mind blossoms with sprouts.... When Anandwan became self-reliant, it completed the second phase of my life's mission. I have reached the half-century of my life wherein I lived with the all-pervading involvement of the caveman... I should have by now become quite complacent and a little detached. But I was more restless than ever,' he says.

This restlessness of Baba led to the opening of another centre for the rehabilitation of the leprosy patients – Ashokwan. For the creation of Ashokwan, land was obtained through a grant from the government of Maharashtra. This land, located on the outskirts of Nagpur, near National Highway No. 7 (NH 7), was spread over a discarded 70 acres. Paradoxically, this land which earlier provided refuge to ex-convicts from Central Jail, was later to become home to another kind of excommunicated men – the diseased and deformed. After the huge efforts of Baba, who worked not 'for' but 'with' his band of these discarded people, this thrown-away land became a spectacle worth witnessing. Ashokwan opened in 1957 with an initial 70 acres, which in 1963 was expanded to 102 acres with the purchase of the adjoining plot of land at the cost of sixteen thousand rupees.

The quietest of the MSS projects, Ashokwan, is chronologically the second centre for the rehabilitation of the leprosy patients. It is managed entirely by the leprosy-handicapped beneficiaries of the MSS, under the supervision of the Anandwan staff. Lying midway between Anandwan and Nagpur, this place is frequently visited by the staff of Anandwan and the visitors travelling between Anandwan and Nagpur. Since Ashokwan falls on the way from Anandwan to Nagpur, the staff and travellers can use it as a resting place. The administration is also easily done in this way.

With the passage of time agriculture has become the mainstay of Ashokwan and it is being entirely managed and run by the cured leprosy patients. Out of a total of 102 acres, 96 acres of land here was fit for cultivation. Cotton is the only cash crop, with fruits like oranges and guavas too chipping in, raising a reasonable income. The dairy and animal husbandry are yet other sources that contribute to the economy even though their contribution is scanty and irregular. Social forestry, which has always been greatly stressed upon by Baba in all his projects, was launched in Ashokwan in 1983 to provide fuel, fodder, timber and bio-fencing. Yet despite all these efforts, Ashokwan, from the looks of it, appears like a foster child. It somehow did not bloom as cheerfully as the other projects despite the best intentions and efforts of all those who participated in its creation. Being thinly populated, it looks a little lonely and abandoned. During times past when Baba was healthy enough to tour all the projects, he would always make it a point to halt at Ashokwan, as to him it was a child that needed encouragement and direction in the course of its development. Even though there are healthy and well-tended-to patches of land to be seen at Ashokwan, it is evident that the magic is missing here that can be seen at any other project of the MSS.

SOMNATH

'What advice Baba? What is your advice to me?' asked the Tibetan spiritual guru, His Holiness the Dalai Lama on his visit to Anandwan. With the calm confidence of age and experience Baba answered him, 'Have faith in your youth. Instil that mighty faith in their hearts. They are our hope. Your tool.' His tremendous, almost blind faith in the capacity of the younger generation was as true a reality to Baba as was the presence of the rising and setting sun in the far horizon. He realized that if the uncontainable physical vigour coupled with an untainted and impressionable mind possessed by a young person were to be taught the values of hard labour, patriotism and selfless service of humanity, it would provide the finest of instruments in fashioning a happier and more livable world, 'to provide new paths of creativity to stop the capabilities of today's angry young generation from going waste and perhaps turning towards destruction.'

'The country is suffering from festering sores. Normal treatments will no more suffice. Unless a problem is understood in all its dimensions, remedy cannot be effective. In place of inspiring ideals one merely sees the sleeping and dying humanity. Unless the youth girdles up its loins to face these problems, a tragedy will become unavoidable,' says Baba.

Such was Baba's faith in the power of the youth that he considered them the only ones capable of averting national tragedies, which were occurring due to the complacency of the older generation. Like so many other initiatives that Baba undertook, while his brethren sighed and blamed their miseries on destiny, this time too he decided to draw up a plan in order to harness this large repository of energy called youth. This plan remained close to his heart for so long that even as he fought to find time off his other projects, it got transformed into a dream. This dream he carried with him as he went about deeply immersed in backbreaking labour in establishing Anandwan, until it almost begged to be converted into a reality. And when Anandwan, which too had begun as a dream, became the most authentic of all realities, Baba's restlessness possessed him once again and he began planning and taking steps towards the realization of the dream that had simmered inside him for a long time. In Baba's mind there were a myriad thoughts and queries that demanded reactions and answers from his own conscience. If one were to follow the trail of these thoughts over the tracks of his own words, it would be possible to understand the reason for the coming into being of the next project. Eager to tap the boundless energy in the youth, Baba went on inventing new ideas.

In 1967, on Baba's request the Maharashtra Government granted to the MSS 1325 acres of land on the edge of a forest reserve. And this was to become the site for the realization of yet another of Baba's noble dreams – a Workers' University. This university was to impart production-oriented education to the youth. It was to be founded on two basic principles expounded by Mahatma Gandhi: one that physical labour leads to the purity of the soul, and second that sufficiency for all must precede superfluity for some. The dream was to bring the healthy and the sick, the educated and the uneducated, the worker and the student, to form a complementary cooperative and creative school for living. It was hoped that by coordinating modern science with the traditions of Indian life, the university would be able to transform the subsisting agriculture into a highly productive agro-industrial system. Baba had expected the Workers' University students to participate in farming, dairy, poultry and agro- based industries and to generate resources while receiving formal education as well. The fees from the students of this university were to be turned into a share in the cooperative system. When the students passed out from this university, they would not only be carrying with them the knowledge and skills of productive life, but also the financial returns on their initial educational investments. For the fulfilment of this goal, a labourers' society, consisting of 25 sturdy and willing young leprosy patients, was formed. They were instructed to take up the arduous task of developing land and water resources in Somnath. On 13th March 1967, fifteen men came to the Somnath jungle to accomplish this goal. Of these fifteen, thirteen were leprosy patients, one Shankar Jumade, and Baba himself.

These are the words in which Baba describes his reasons for and the journey towards achievement of his goal of the Workers' University:

> An era of disenchantment and frustration knocked on the door. The old beliefs had crashed and crumbled and the new ones had not been formed.... Just one mighty push across the Himalayas and all our mansions of self-delusions crumpled. We faced the world with our poverty totally exposed.'
>
> Afflicted by mental leprosy, my country scampered in every direction begging like a leprosy patient and this picture of my country was enough to totally tear to shreds any person's mental detachment.
>
> Why did this happen? What was the remedy for it? My dream for

> the Workers' University started where I reached in search of the basic replies to these posers and on the shoulders of Anandwan experiment. This restless search symbolizes the evolution in my life. 'Not to loiter when once you reach a peak but to start the search for new peaks,' was my motto, since resting at a peak marks the beginning of a slide-down.

Obtaining the land and ridding it of wild undergrowth, boulders and other hazards that nature had created was the easiest work in the face of another fiercer hurdle that obstructed the path leading to the establishment of the university. This hurdle was man-made. For a long time the villagers of the surrounding areas had been using the jungle land of Somnath that was granted to the MSS. They had since 1957 encroached upon about 500–600 acres of this land and had been using it as a pathway for fodder, fuel, leaves and grass for thatching huts, and wood for making agricultural instruments. When Baba, along with his army of fifteen patients, landed here and began digging, cutting and tilling this land, the villagers rose in protest against them. Their reasons being two: firstly, they would be deprived of the land on which they were heavily dependant; and secondly, they were both terrorized as well as raged on learning that this land would be used by people suffering from a most dreadful disease on account of which they had been socially ostracized. They could not contemplate living in the neighbourhood of social outcasts. So, they retaliated. Under the leadership of a local leader, the villagers rose in rebellion, opposing the presence of Baba and his team by staging a number of 'Satyagrahas'. These 'Satyagrahas' started turning violent as more and more people began joining them till the situation became extremely volatile. Baba tried to pacify the farmers by returning 600 acres of land to the government but the agitations continued unabated. They had yet another demand. They demanded that they be allowed to use the waters of a perennial spring called 'Umri Zhara' flowing from the mountain slopes of Somnath. The Somnath workers had built a temporary traversable bridge over this spring, which, they alleged, prevented the water from going into the neighbouring fields. For the next three years Somnath became shrouded in controversies in which a number of leaders too intervened in order to bring about some kind of truce. Finally Baba realized the futility of wasting time by keeping engaged in a seemingly solutionless tussle. All controversies were silenced when Baba conceded to the demands of the villagers by signing an agreement countersigned by Vinoba. According to the pact of the agreement, the MSS was to distribute 145 acres of land amongst the landless villagers and to leave the waters of the perennial spring untouched. The end of the conflict came at a heavy price. Baba's dream of the Workers' University was thwarted. But to thwart Baba's enthusiasm was impossible. Putting behind him the pain of the three years during which he fought for his dream project, Baba set down to convert Somnath into a purely agricultural project. So astounding was the outcome that today Somnath has become a model for agricultural development. No lesser achievement could be imagined when so exalted were the intentions of Baba, 'Now the welcome arches denoting the boundaries of a new homestead have to be erected where revolutions will take shape to vanquish the armies of poverty, while the heads carrying loads will rise higher than the spires of churches, the heads of visionaries will also bow before those who write the epics on the face of the earth with the furrows of their ploughs,' he enivisioned.

Undaunted by the death of a dear dream and urged on by his innate restlessness, Baba hit upon yet another idea – that of organizing youth camps. This idea was based on his faith in youth power and his belief that it could be tapped and tutored to achieve big goals in life. After the forest had been cleared, the land tilled, the roads laid, buildings constructed and wells dug by the leprosy patients who had accompanied Baba, the first youth camp was organized in 1967. The basic ideals and objectives of these youth camps covered a wide rage, from personality development and character building to realizing the force and importance of organized action in the best interests of the community and the nation. Baba felt that the youth needed not only inspiration, but also affection and understanding to achieve the ideals. 'Let them once taste the joy of organized endeavour and they will come to realize that the gap between thought and deed has to be bridged first.' He also felt that the younger generation should come out of the cocoon of the academic life and face as well as participate in the real groundwork, which will prepare them better for life – its duties and responsibilities both. These youth camps are held regularly every summer at Somnath for ten days and are attended by a thousand young people. They live for ten days in sweltering heat, learning to live without luxuries and comforts that they take for granted in their daily lives and thus are able to understand the large gaps in the rural and urban settings. They eat simple food at fixed times without frills, in contrast to the gluttony that some of us indulge in at times. The day ends with discussions and group activities and the young ones go to bed with a conscience which has been jolted and awoken to unrecognized but bitter realities. These youth camps have been modelled on the concept of 'Antar Bharti' or united India, set forth by Baba's mentor Sane Guruji.

Young men and women from different parts of India participate in intense physical labour called 'Shramdan'. Till the time Baba was able to attend and supervise these camps, these youngsters got an opportunity to stay with Baba and know and learn from him. But now even though Baba can no longer be there because of ill-health and old age, the eagerness and enthusiasm of the youth of India to participate in the youth camps has not dimmed. The assembled youth contributing the 'gift of labour', or 'Shramdan', and getting exposed to the toil and sweat of rural masses belonged to both the urban and rural classes. The experience of some of these youth was so enduring that they decided to stay there and contribute to the social welfare activities being carried out. Two such young men are Jaggannath and Arun Kadam, both of whom attended the youth camp in 1973–74, stayed on and now are maintaining the Nagepalli and Somnath projects respectively. Today Somnath is a fully thriving agricultural wonder, which follows the same successful pattern of Anandwan as regards community living, medical services and rehabilitation of the handicapped.

Baba knew that to improve the country's prospects youth power had to be harnessed. Thus he dreamed of setting up a Workers' University. But the pursuit of this dream ended up in the establishment of Somnath. 'When a sick society enters an age of uncertainty, something has to be done quickly. Our aim is to prove that something can actually be done, even against odds.' Despite this dream dying before it could be born, Baba was not among those to stop and suffer. 'I treat my capacity to treat failures as my biggest strength, a blessing of nature. Though such failures may evoke derisive laughter, they do not bring disappointment, remorse or take my breath away through setbacks. These small failures help me find the right direction.' It was this confidence that finally led to the success of Somnath.

CHAPTER 9

Hemalkasa and Base Camp Nagepalli

The woods are lovely dark and deep
But I have promises to keep
And miles to go before I sleep.

This piece of poetry is the creation of one of the greatest poets of all times, Robert Frost, but it was Baba who truthfully upheld the essence of these lines by *actually* living them. He literally trudged over miles and miles of barren stretches, facing challenges to illumine empty hearts, promising to bring order into a deteriorating value system.

By the end of the nineteen sixties and the beginning of the seventies, Somnath had become a fully functional agricultural unit and Baba realized it. 'Anandwan has become a reality long back. My presence is no more needed even at Somnath now' and 'My mind however races ahead. The body is no longer able to keep pace with it. And so I become restless and search for youth to help me.' These musings were indicative of two things. Firstly, the innate restlessness had gripped Baba again and he was already in the process of looking for other problems to be solved and more people to be served. Secondly, years of indulging in hard physical labour was beginning to take a toll on his health. He began realizing that he would have to search for younger bones and blood to carry forward the task which he had begun. The next project he had in mind was based on the experience of his teenage days. During adolescence his sneaky trips into the virgin forests of the Gadchiroli District, during his summer vacations, led him to the tribals living in those forests. Along with fascination for their indigenous lifestyle, stark honesty and immense physical endurance, Baba was also pained by the exploitation of these innocent, unassuming people at the hands of the urban elite and their living of poor unhealthy lives on account of ignorance. The wound inflicted by this pain perhaps never healed because many decades later, having the success stories of Anandwan and Somnath behind him, he felt empowered enough to fight for their rights to a healthy and happy existence. It was with this aim in mind that Baba, during the spring of 1971, led an adventure group belonging to Antarbharti (a youth organization), to Bhamragarh situated deep in the Gadchiroli forests located in the heart of Central India. About the adventure he says: 'The adventure trip to Bhamragadh was an invitation as well as a challenge for the youth. There would be an opportunity to enjoy life and also face challenges. They would know more closely their brethren rotting in poverty, exploited by deception and downtrodden by injustice.'

In the winter of 1973, Baba organized a trek for his wife and three children. Dr. Prakash Amte, the younger of the two sons of Baba and Tai, recalls, 'His aim was to see the effect on us two brothers, of the plight of the tribals. He cleverly disguised his aim under the pleasant garb of a trek. But we were all as equally shocked on seeing their condition as Baba had been when he'd seen them for the first time.' The family camped under the canopy of a large benevolent mango tree and was made to sleep on the bare ground. When they saw for themselves the almost sub-human living standards of the Madia-Gond tribals, it was Prakash who was moved the most. He was at that time awaiting the results of his MBBS degree, but he had his mind made up – to dedicate himself to the service of these innocent people by utilizing all his medical expertise. Baba's job was done and he returned to Anandwan a very happy but ill man. He had to be rushed to London for a major surgical operation on his spinal cord. His dear sister Lila was the one who arranged his trip and was by his bedside along with Tai.

Meanwhile, back home Prakash had already decided to seek allotment of the land by the government, in order to start work in the Bhamragadh jungles. Bhamragadh is in the tribal area forming a part of the Gadchiroli District of Maharashtra, Andhra Pradesh and Madhya Pradesh. This is a delta of the seven rivers – Bandiya, Pearlkota, Pamuli Gautmi, Indravati, Pranahita, Vainganga and Godvari. 'This must have been the land,' Baba thinks, 'that tempted the sages to write the Vedas.' It was in 1971 that a formal application was made to the government of Maharashtra state, requesting for the land adjoining the river, so that the tribals could be trained in agricultural operations, of which they were entirely ignorant. The only food that they consumed was roots of some plants and whatever moved on land on its four legs! The government however dillydallied and took two years to finally grant the request for land, and the land offered was three kilometres away from the river. Prakash was in a fix, but he had to come to some decision in the absence of both his parents, who at that time were in London for Baba's operation. He decided to take up the offer. On 23rd December 1973, the actual possession of the land was received and the 'Lok Biradri Prakalp' (LBP) or 'The People's Brotherhood Project', envisioned by Baba, came into existence at Hemalkasa, two miles from Bhamragadh.

This project began initially as a five-day programme, in which five young workers with a rich repository of varied experiences and ideas would participate. A jeep or station wagon would carry both provisions and the workers to the area on weekdays. These workers were to set up camp in a far-away area, as the tribals were mistrusting and wary of the people of the outside world. Each worker was required to delve into the collection of his rich experiences and then try to first tempt and then to slowly win the confidence of the tribals. And finally these young workers, after gaining the trust of the tribals, could go and live among them to teach them about agriculture, health and the like and in turn learn from them about their rich and unique culture and language. Of these five young enthusiasts, three were: a young Dr. Prakash Amte, freshly out of the medical college at Nagpur, his wife Dr. Mandakini and Renuka, Baba's daughter. All three realized the enormity and the complexity of the task that they had volunteered for. But when they saw the abject poverty and isolation of the tribals, their resolve to fulfil this task was only further strengthened.

The Madia Gond tribals had been living isolated, in stark poverty and malnutrition and with a high incidence of diseases like tuberculosis, malaria, leprosy, dysentery, etc. Their culture, having been far beyond the precincts of modern civilization, was very traditional, but their lives were very hard. They clung to their superstitions with almost a fierce possessiveness, as they knew of no other way of life. Besides, the terrain too presented numerous challenges to these people. They died not only from disease, starvation, superstitious practices and lack of facilities, but also from other dangers like wild animals and reptiles, wildfires, storms and floods. Doctors and medicines were unheard-of here. They relied on deities to cure them, and not many were able to survive beyond the age of forty.

The sunburned Madia women are wide-nosed, thick-lipped, bare-chested, with a wrap covering their lower bodies. Long strings of chunky ornaments made of stones, beads, etc. hang around their necks, providing some cover to their bare upper bodies. The menfolk are nude except for the jock straps that they wear. The children scamper about without any shred of clothing.

Braving hazards such as severe winters, scorching summers, lack of even the basic amenities like electricity, roads, transport, etc., and attack by wild animals and Naxalites, the party of the five brave young people set up camp under a thatched hut. The going was very tough. The tribals mistrusted the Amtes' intentions, since they had always only been exploited, either by forest officials or Naxalites or other civilians. But none of the five lost heart. They tried to learn the language of the tribals and urged them to take medicines rather than look to their deities to cure them. Then one day Prakash revived a dying patient of malaria, and that day a bond was born between the tribals and the LBP workers. Word got around in the tribal neighbourhood and soon dozens of tribals began flocking the foliage-roofed and bamboo supported dormitories that had been constructed for the sick and the convalescents. The hospital began with a leaf-thatched hut as accommodation for patients who travelled from far and near on foot, by bullock carts or dugouts, in all stages of various kinds of illnesses. An adjoining shed served as a surgical tent and a wooden bench outside was used to examine, cut open abscesses, dress wounds and give medicines. The doctor duo of Prakash and Manda went from village to village treating rheumatism, leprosy, cirrhosis of the liver, etc. Then in 1975, Dr. Schnellman, of the Swiss Aid Abroad, paid a visit to Hemalkasa and stayed there for two days in a hut. Moved by conditions in which work was being done, he offered to fund the construction of some buildings – houses, godowns and a hospital. This helped immensely, giving a quantum leap to the work being carried out at Hemalkasa. Things became more ordered, comfortable, and hence more efficient. Now remained the problem of electricity. For twenty years there had been no electricity here. Broken bones were set without X-rays and surgery was carried out under the light of kerosene lamps! And when finally electricity did come with a promise of wiping out the darkness, it was extremely erratic. Textbook treatment was not always possible because patients often came in advanced stages of illnesses and also because facilities were rudimentary. One thing about the Madiyas that Prakash says he has always marvelled at is their extreme physical endurance. These people, he says, have a tremendous capacity to withstand pain and suffering. From many incidents Prakash recounts a few that exemplify this quality: Once a man, while hunting with his friends, was attacked by a bear. His scalp was split open and he was even blinded, but the man walked to the hospital in that state! In another instance, a baby's head got stuck in the mother's womb during childbirth. The mother asked Prakash to chop off the child's head, which he did but with reluctance. Another woman had her intestines spilled out when she was attacked by some wild animal. This woman walked to the hospital holding her intestines and walked back home after having them tucked and sewed back in place!

But now things have improved. In addition to a hospital, there is a dormitory of concrete, for less serious patients and the attendants of the serious ones. A very spacious room has been built for the examination of the patients. Twice a week free meals are given to the patients. Many machines, gadgets and medicines are now available. Dr. Digant (Prakash's son), Dr. Kanna Dobi and Dr. Pandu Pungati (Madiya tribals) have joined the hospital and relieved Prakash and Manda of some burden.

On April 14, 2003, I reach Hemalkasa from Anandwan. After passing through the entrance of the LBP this is the scene that emerges like a mirage, out of nowhere in the wilderness – brick and tile structures, old, new and unfinished, interspersed with tall green trees and a barrage of bougainvilleas in varied hues, spread over a very large clearing. Sounds of the jungle – monkey squeals, lion roars, jackal howls, dog barks and peacock screeches – greet me. At the entrance of Prakash's house an immensely warm welcome is extended by Prakash, Manda and Tai while Baba is resting. What better culmination could I have asked for to a long arduous journey through the forest? Prakash and Manda's home is a simple, double-storied, concrete structure, the entrance to which is overhung by an enormous bougainvillea bush, in full pink bloom. My twin bedroom on the first floor of the house is unpretentious and comfortable. There are no charges for boarding, lodging and meals! The Amte hospitality is unique.

My next day is packed with a trip to the Animal Orphanage, with Prakash as my guide. First he tells me the story behind the beginning of the Animal Orphanage. One day while wandering in the jungle, Prakash saw some tribals who were returning from a hunting spree. They had killed two Bonnet Macaques (a kind of monkey) and were carrying them slung on a rod. One of them was a female and to her breast was clinging a baby Macaque, which was still alive. Moved by the sight, Prakash persuaded the tribals to give him the baby. Over the next two days he bottle- fed the monkey and soon it forgot its own mother and came to regard Prakash as its mother. Prakash called it Babli, after the tribal deity, Babli. Babli went on to become the first inmate of the Animal Orphanage at Hemalkasa. When the tribals saw Prakash's love for animals, they began bringing to him all orphaned, diseased and hurt animals as gifts, by way of gratitude towards their beloved doctor. The members of the LBP had no expertise on rearing animals but their affection for the animals enabled them to transcend their lack of training.

Just outside the entrance to Prakash's house there is a cage inside which two fawns wobble around. They are a rare 'barking deer' species. I am handed a bottle of milk to feed them and soon they are merrily sucking on it in turns. We move ahead, to the back of the house. Till now a faint rumble that had hung in the air becomes clearly decipherable as the roar of a lion. In a few minutes we are at the lion's den. The thing that strikes one is the cleanliness of the den, which is free of the foul raw-meat odour, of even the best of zoos in the world. Prakash opens a small back door to the cage and jumps in. The three beasts, Negal and Negali (male and female leopards) and a lion, rush to him wagging their tails like tame dogs. Soon they are one happy family – Mr. and Mrs. Negal, the lion and Prakash. With his fist curled and comfortably lodged between the jaws of the lion, Prakash strokes the majestic leopard couple with his other hand. His look of genuine affection confirms the truth of his assertion, 'I'm their mother. I have reared them and they'd die before even scratching me.' Then throwing them large chunks of meat he jumps out of the cage, slowly closing and locking the door after him. Thereafter, we move from cage to cage spread haphazardly between the various buildings of the LBP, as if they had been built in emergency, in whatever space was available. All orphaned, abandoned and hurt animals brought here by the tribals are revived and reared by Prakash and his team. This accounts for the happy sounds of the jungle that greet one on entering Hemalkasa. Love abounds here – the sight of a bitch suckling a kitten, a monkey riding on the back of a dog, deadly grisly bears drooling over Prakash's hands, crocodiles responding to his whistling and lions and tigers wagging their tails like tame dogs on seeing him are very common sights. Today the list of animals at the LBP Animal Orphanage is inexhaustible: leopards, lions, barking deer, mouse deer, chameleons, nilgai (blue Indian bull), otters, wild boars, hyenas, vipers, cobras, kraits, owls, eagles, civet cats, crocodiles and monkeys. All the animals are in excellent health and hence the envy of both the forest officials and the zoo-keepers. Prakash has even given a number of lion cubs and various other animals to the local zoo. Despite this the LBP was being penalized for holding animals 'illegally'. The government was threatening to take the animals away and giving them to the local zoo. In February 2003, Prakash threatened to return the Padmashri which he had received for rendering exemplary service to the tribals of Bhamragadh. The threat worked. Now the government has given permission to the LBP to keep and maintain the animals but has asked them to build a zoo, away from the living quarters, since as of now the cages of the animals lie interspersed amongst the houses of the LBP workers, but the animals however have never caused any harm to the people. The cost of building a zoo, says Prakash, will be staggering. He has requested a number of national and international social service and funding organizations to come to his rescue. The going will again be tough but having inherited fortitude from his illustrious father, Prakash remains undaunted by the task and hopeful of its success.

When the LBP was started, there was no plan to run a school. The plan was dictated by circumstances. Prakash and the others realized that the only way the tribals could escape exploitation and know of their rights was through education. In addition to reading and writing, agricultural techniques, healthcare and hygiene were also essentials that were required to be taught. With this in view, a residential school was started in 1976. Gopal Phadnis, the principal since 1976, recalls how he and some other members of the LBP, went from village to village entreating the parents to send their children to school. By this time the hospital had been functioning for three years, and the Amtes had become well-known. But the Madias were still suspicious, not of the LBP people, but of education. Finally some of them relented, not for the sake of education, but because of the meals their children would get at the school and also because they would get medicines and improved agricultural training, through their children. Prakash says, 'We were not bothered about government grant or recognition, but about the enrolment of the Madiya children and their continuing to study. We were planning about how to make the children want to come and stay and how to make their parents send them.' This was however not the last or the least of the difficulties, problem after problem stood staring the LBP workers in the eye: the textbooks were all in Marathi and the Madias spoke a language that had no script. And as if this was not enough, the children often ran away from school and had to be chased and brought back. But despite all these hardships no one gave up. Plans were devised and paths were built in a wilderness of problems. Standard textbooks were discarded. The LBP people began learning in Madiya language common words and concepts and names of objects – living and non-living. Then the children were taught these in Marathi. Languages were learned in the old barter system technique, words exchanged for words, concepts for concepts and objects for objects. The system worked. The children began getting the hang of it and stopped running away from school. Efforts blossomed, word spread and slowly the strength of the students in the school began increasing. The school that started in 1976 with 32 boys and three girls today has 500 students, most of them boarders, with many thousands already having passed out of the school. The school has a tightly packed schedule, as there is so much for the children to learn and only so little time for it. The morning instruction consists of formal learning, and the afternoons are devoted to practical training in agriculture, carpentry, iron-smithy, etc. During vacations each child takes home a packet of seeds for their kitchen gardens, which they have taught their parents to rear and tend. The children are made to grow and eat their own produce even at school so that they can convince their parents about the values of advanced agriculture. In the last almost three decades since the school was started, some of the children who have passed out from here have either taken up teaching as a profession, or pursued sports. Two of them are doctors who now work at the hospital at Hemalkasa, trying to repay some of their debt to the institution that gave them the gift of education. Three decades of selfless service of Prakash and Mandakini have not gone unrewarded. They are referred to as the Schweitzer couple of India and in 1995, the generous Prince of Monaco (Europe), issued a postage stamp in their name, in order to honour them. The Indian government has honoured them with Padmashri.

And what does Baba think of the efforts of his son Prakash and daughter-in-law Manda, who took up the challenge to serve the Madias and made a success of Baba's endeavour? 'I think I am as proud as any other father would be of his children. I am as human as any, capable of emotions, of committing errors and succeeding. Why do you think I would react any differently than any other man?'

NAGEPALLI

In 1973–74 a young boy Jagannath Mechkale attended the youth camp at Somnath, which, little did he know, would change his outlook on life as well as the course of his life. Jagannath, at that time a college-going student of economics, was so impressed by Baba's ideals and work that he made up his mind to stay on at Somnath and help out in any capacity that he could. He remembers with a far-away look that had a slight suggestion of sadness, 'During those days we had a lot of enthusiasm. We, the younger lot, wanted to contribute to something worthwhile. We wanted action, we were ready for any kind of physical labour and any other challenge. And we found it all at Somnath.' And about Baba, 'Well it is difficult to explain the feeling, one had to experience being with him and surrendering oneself to his ideals and inspiration. We were mesmerized by his words. He looked like a lion with such fire in his words, that we....' And he just trails off again into the past, not finding appropriate words to express the emotions of his youth. 'Anyway I told my family that I wanted to stay with Baba and take part in the work that Baba was doing. My family did not take it nicely, they tried all kinds of blackmail to get me back, but my mind was made up and nothing could shake my conviction. So I left home and began work at Anandwan, Somnath, anywhere that my services were needed and of any kind.'

When the plan for setting up of the LBP was drawn up, it was felt that a base camp was a necessity for this project. During monsoons the rivers would get furious and spread havoc, flooding and clogging the jungle path through the forests of Bhamragadh, cutting off Hemalkasa for months together. For this purpose 20 acres of land was obtained at Nagepalli from the state government. This land is situated 3km from the Nagepalli village, and Jagannath was sent there to start and supervise the proceedings of the base camp. He recalls fondly the days when he, along with Baba and Tai, stayed initially in a single thatched hut, which served as a kitchen as well. And then another hut of the same kind was made to shift Jagannath and some other workers into it. Jagan, as he is popularly known, remembers that Baba and Tai would stay for days at Nagepalli, on their way to Hemalkasa (on foot!) and instruct and inspire them for running the base camp. Tai would cook for all of them and feed them like her own sons. In those days Nagepalli served only as a base where people from other projects carrying rations, medicines, etc. would break journey in order to rest before proceeding to Hemalkasa. But gradually Jagan and the others there started growing vegetables and food grains for their sustenance. The extra that was produced, they began selling in the village. Encouraged by their success in agriculture they started a small dairy and poultry project. Today Nagepalli remains not a mere base camp but a self-reliant, independent unit. Jagan and his wife have shifted into a small concrete building, which is their home as well as a rest house to those going to Hemalkasa. Food is cooked by Jagan's wife and the hospitality of the couple is incomparable to any that at least I have experienced.

CHAPTER 10

The Inside Story of His Mentors and Motivations

Baba is an enigma which has escaped the confines of definition, for the simple reason that he possesses a mature sense of purpose in addition to a methodology free from ideological shackles. He is as devout a Hindu as any other, the best Christian that can be and a greatly enlightened Buddhist who possesses the purity of a Muslim – and yet he pursues only one religion ardently – Work.

> My work is my pulpit. God has given me one mouth, but two hands. I'm preaching with my hands… for me there is no better religion than the one that builds inside human beings a sense of dignity and self-esteem. I am glad that this definition of religion seems acceptable. I am not religious, traditionally speaking, but I feel religion is that force which builds a stronger and more righteous human being.

This much is then clear, that religion cannot pride itself for having influenced, motivated or driven Baba. He almost appears an agnostic, who does not acknowledge the existence of an empty God – a God who is a preacher of purposeless directives that men have gathered and strung together like a garland called religion and which they then carry around their necks as burdens. He would rather any day choose to bow his head on the altar of a man who follows no other religion but honest dedication to his work. In a country like India where people draw life-breath for existence from religion, where from, then, does this one man extract his fuel that drives him and keeps the fire of his conviction burning? Where from, if not religion? Some excerpts from Baba's Magsaysay Award speech holds the answer to this one:

> I never wanted to commit 'the Sin' of turning a deaf ear to the plaintive cries of thousands of leprosy patients, of people who were physically handicapped, who, though present in the world, are absent – the deaf, mute youth united only in the fraternity of frustration... people whose intestines were gnawed by hunger, whose minds were darkened by ignorance and hatred, whose eyes opened into perpetual night, tribals who remained unprotesting for an agonizingly long time....
>
> My love for these people cleansed my polluted heart, sanctified my ambitions, sweetened my relationships, glorified my undertakings and transformed the shadows into bursting dawn of the eternal day of my life.
>
> Those walking in the twilight of life, those seeking honestly the last harvest in their lives, those desiring with shaky confidence to add new life to their years, those leading lives of loneliness – I wanted to be their companion, in their long lonely voyages of life....
>
> I wanted to be the contemporary to those. 'Lords of conspicuous scars' – Christ, Damien, Gandhi. I saw the imprint of those nails with which Christ was crucified, on the palms of Damien and on the breast of Gandhi. Every time I see the imprint of Christ's kiss on his forehead.

So it was men in pain and need, who moved Baba, who knocked on his conscience, who awoke his latent sensibilities and drove him to plunge into action, the result of which was the creation of as monumental a work as Anandwan, 'Our poem in action', as Baba refers to it. Meaningless religious dogmas expounded by conceited high priests of religion... these were not able to leave the tiniest mark, leave alone an influence on a man made of unique mettle. And this is his message, 'God has been divided by temples, mosques and churches. The land has been divided and even the sea. Let us not divide man.' For Baba spirituality is not the otherworldly. It is an introspective search for an order in an individual and the universe and when the search is turned outward it is a science. Despite his non-adherence to various forms of religiosity, he fully respects the religious beliefs of others. One need not go a long way in search for the proof of this – the secular lifestyle practised at Anandwan, which is always open to all kinds of visitors at all hours, is all that needs to be witnessed. Furthermore, Baba has always had sincere empathy for the religious fervour of his own wife, Sadhana Tai, and daughters-in-law – Dr. Bharti and Dr. Mandakini – who are forever engaged in acts of piety, through the observance of fasts and performance of rigorous prayers. At one time there were rumours that Baba picked flowers every day for his wife's daily prayers. When Tai was confronted about this, she clearly refuted the rumours with a shy chuckle, saying, 'Catch Baba bringing flowers for me everyday. He brought them only once.' Another story, a true one though, goes thus: once as Baba waited with a friend of his, while Tai was performing her prayers, he said good-humouredly, 'Let her finish. She is praying for both of us.'

It is difficult to describe Baba in a few sentences. He is a man of contradictions – a visionary and a realist at the same time; tough and unyielding, but also soft and kind to the outcast and exploited. On the one hand he is a poet, and on the other, a rough-hewn rustic, who has done such menial chores as scavenging, well-digging and wood-chopping, follows simple living but high thinking. Different people use different words to describe him but he says only this about himself, 'I want to be known as a social mechanic who goes round with an oil can to lubricate difficult human situations and thus make them better.'

MAHATMA GANDHI

During the nineteen thirties and forties, Baba was no different from the youth of the country of that time – he too like them became fascinated with the philosophy of Gandhi, which offered a solution to rid the country of British imperialism. But the similarity between Baba and his contemporaries can be carried no further. He remained to the very last, the only one who not only upheld but practised and put to test most of Gandhi's ideals, which to skeptics were as insane as the man himself. An interesting as well as unseemly comparison is sometimes drawn between the Guru and the disciple, that both are insane. Baba's commitment to his work was beyond the bindings of width, depth and heights. He was a man in a hurry to fulfil his mission and achieve results. His zeal and vitality made it difficult for him to pause and explain his vision to others. This attitude of his led some to find a streak of mental abnormality in him, which they claimed he inherited from his partly demented mother. However, for a man like him who is not 'a man in general' but a 'General' amongst men, it is usual to be both extraordinary and abnormal at the same time. And of his mentor Gandhi, Erik Erickson has said that in the Mahatma, the abnormal and the supernormal vie with disarming frankness. This comparison between Baba and Gandhi could likewise be drawn between any other men of similar statures, whose actions and their meanings are sometimes beyond the comprehension of common people like us. Many other similarities between the lives of these exalted men can be drawn – their renunciation of a prospective law career, belief in and adherence to following a simple lifestyle, emphasis on decentralization, empathy with the outcast and downtrodden and preference of agriculture and cottage industries over urban industrialization.

With the return of Gandhi to India from South Africa, the face of India's politics changed radically. The faith in the armed revolution was becoming shaky. The policy of making moderate appeals to the British Parliament was becoming unviable. The Tilak era was coming to an end. The news about the communist revolution in Russia was generating new hopes. Britain was determined not to lose its hold on power and there were apparent signs that the First World War would soon come to an end. This atmosphere of hope prompted Gandhi to launch his weapons of non-violence and Satyagraha, which he had developed and tested in South Africa. Increasing importance was being attached to constructive work and social service. Several new schemes of social rejuvenation were begun, new centres were opened to operate these schemes and hundreds of workers were absorbed into them. Till then, the service to leprosy patients was the monopoly of Christian missionaries, but in 1936, with the efforts of Gandhi and Vinoba, Maharogi Sewa Mandal was established, and in 1941 a leprosy home was started at Dattapur (near Gandhi's Wardha Ashram). Besides this, Gandhi's eleven codes of personal behaviour too gripped the imagination of thousands of Indians, and among them one was Murlidhar Devidas Amte. Further, Gandhi's strong sense of responsibility, an acute sense of justice, belief in self, tempered with compassion, determination and the mastering of fear were the latent attributes of Baba's character too and which were awoken under the strong influence of his mentor. It became evident from his actions from 1935 onwards that Baba had chosen Gandhi as his guiding star. His conviction was firm, 'If the world of have-nots is to survive, Gandhiji's path has no alternative.' He who had at one time held a firm belief that an armed revolution was the only way to wrest freedom from the imperialists now began speaking a different language, 'Revolution is not linked to destruction, but to creation. Its face is not smeared with blood but suffused with sweat.'

Baba's *Shramashram* or 'Cooperative Labour Commune' project, was Gandhian thought put to practice. From the ruins of this project was created another sublime centre – Anandwan – for the service of the needy and this too was based on Gandhi's philosophy of service to one's fellow-beings. 'Consciously or unconsciously, every one of us does render some service or other. If we cultivate the habit of doing this service deliberately, our desire for service will steadily grow stronger, and will make not only for our own happiness but that of the world at large' (M.K. Gandhi).

Baba the poet has paid a glowing tribute to his hero through beautiful words:

His prominent rib-cage
displayed two medals of honour
And being a naked mendicant
They were pinned to his flesh

One of it was pain
And the other faith.
Pain symbolized of today
And faith a promise of tomorrow
Till his end, between the banks
of pain and faith
flowed this saint's life-stream
but it also had a third bank
of eternity
which had bestowed right from the beginning
maturity
having this maturity alone
makes the burden of prophethood bearable
and the face bears permanently
that childlike smile
which is a sign of a prophet's humanity.

Despite all the inspiration that Baba had drawn from the Gandhian ideals and however much he had attempted to establish all ventures he attempted on those ideals, he is his own man. He has principles and values that are distinctly his own. His fierce individuality and originality is a very visible trait, which one does not fail to notice on encountering the man. 'The two greats of Sewagram and Shantiniketan, with whom I was fortunate to live, quarreled with them both, loved them immensely and also earned their love.' Although others have labelled him as the 'last true Gandhian' and Baba acknowledges the inspiration he received, he believes, 'We should avoid tutelage to any dogma or to any one leader, past or present.'

VINOBA BHAVE

Apart from Gandhi, Vinoba Bhave was the man whose ideals Baba adopted and followed. He was also the man who gave Baba courage and comfort during testing times. Baba held deep respect for Vinoba.

In *The Man and His Mission* by S.M. Shirodkar and Dr. B.G. Bapat, the writers have explicitly written of Baba's relationship with Vinoba: 'Vinoba was another role model. After the forced closure of the Cooperative Labour Commune (*Shramashram*), Vinoba had provided solace to Baba. Later on he had also inaugurated the Anandwan project. At the time of many difficult turns and twists in life, Baba had taken counsel from Vinoba and unhesitatingly accepted his decisions *in toto*.' In one of the poems in *Karunecha Kalam* (A Charter of Empathy, a collection of Baba's poems), he thus addresses Vinoba:

> Your soothing hand caressing backs shaking with grief
> when you moved over my back, my pains became blessed.
> You said, 'You are the truth.
> Behind your unity will gather the ciphers.'
> You were the first ray of rising sun in my life
> And the golden glow of the evening
> Is illuminating the paths of my dreams.

In Baba's opinion, when the country became orphaned, devastated and leaderless after Gandhiji's assassination, Vinoba brought a ray of hope and light to the nation. So Baba says of him:

> When the invincible superman fell to the madman's bullet
> amidst the cries of those cursing the darkness
> a wick-lamp glowing with self-sacrifice
> we saw in your skinny body,
> and those stumbling in darkness
> found reassuring light.

When violence exploded after the partition and it was felt that its economic problems will ruin the country, Vinoba attacked the refugee problem in Delhi. Later, he went to Telangana in Andhra Pradesh, after the communist uprising there. He moved on foot all over to study the problem at first hand. He brought forth an extraordinary, unheard-of, novel solution to the land problem in India in the form of 'Bhoodan' (voluntary renunciation of landholding). He undertook a walking tour of the four corners of the country for twelve years. The movement of 'Bhoodan' (offering one's ancestral lands as a gift to the nation) swept throughout the country and led many to believe it to be the beginning of a bloodless revolution. The whole nation was electrified. Baba saw Vinoba of that time thus:

> When in the south, singing, 'Sabai bhoomi Gopal ki' (all land vests in God)
> you surged forth alone
> like the only saint of the Upanishad period
> wearing the embellishment of asceticism,
> searching out the broken strands of lost empathy
> patching, stitching the torn skies
> containing the storm of adventure in broken ribs
> you marched through the raging violence,
> at that time we saw
> the invincible strength of your legs
> and devotion to God in heavenly dreams.

But 'Bhoodan' proved to be a passing phase, ebbing as fast as it crested. Lakhs of acres of land were offered in 'Bhoodan', which was a unique occurrence in world history. The idea of 'Bhoodan' was further widened in 'Gramdan' (gift of a village), 'Jiladan' (gift of a district) and 'Prakhand' (gift of a region). At this juncture, even though he was assisted by a large number of selfless workers, Vinoba withdrew from all public programmes into himself. Baba writes,

> Instead of withdrawing into total seclusion, he should have made his public programmes more broad-based. The land revolution envisaged by him could not have been achieved merely by pledges on paper or passage of Gramdan Act. The sparks generated at different places should have been consolidated by these workers through thousands of projects developing them into a raging inferno. He should have also undertaken a plan to channelize the power generated through 'Bhoodan'

movement into other creative programmes. Removing the blindfold of past prejudices and discarding ritualistic activities, these workers should have waged war on the front of land revolution. They should have managed projects from natural farming to mechanized farming and from cottage-based spinning wheels to cooperative spinning mills. The self-deluding tendency of enjoying the benefits of industrialization as well as treating giant machinery as a curse had to be given up. The peacekeeping army of Vinoba should have finally joined farming projects because peace is not achieved through intellectual enlightenment and cannot survive on an empty stomach.

Baba was hopeful about the possibilities inherent in 'Bhoodan' and 'Gramdan' movements. But Vinoba withdrew into himself, and it ended any experimentation and assessment of future possibilities. A revolution arrived with all fanfare and faded ignominiously into the annals of historic failures.
So Baba posed the question to Vinoba:

May I ask you?
You changed impossibility into possibility
And converted possibility into probability
When the journey towards universal acceptability was
To start
Why did you think of
The escapist luxury of withdrawal?

Baba failed to understand Vinoba's actions and reaction in respect of Sarvodya and several important events in the country, and so he asks:

You gave a national pledge of Sarvodya
the tree flowered, blossomed
but bore no fruit.
Why?
Claiming allegiance to the soil, you roamed
Like a wandering encyclopedia
And were the seismograph of the public mind

> But you withdrew within yourself
> To become immune to nearby earthquake!
> Why did your natural sensitivity become dead?

And this last one:

> So logical in all personal matters why were you so soft and indulgent towards others?
> The questions were unending...
> For the welfare of all, groping in the dark
> Why should you alone shoulder the burden?

SANE GURUJI

Sane Guruji was a local writer, patriot and a freedom fighter whom Baba never came into direct contact with, but the Guru's service-orientation, self-sacrificing nature, immense empathy for the have-nots and the untouchables, indomitable will and fearlessness to stake his life in a fight against injustice and his immense faith in the capability of the youth deeply impressed Baba. So great was Baba's love for Sane Guruji that he commenced many of his works on 24th December, the latter's birthday! Baba considers the inspiration collected from Sane Guruji's book on Indian culture and his life in general a debt:

> Just as flowers and fruits cannot define the debt that they owe to the sun, I owe a similar wordless debt to him. I knew him not while he lived but had merely seen him only once from a distance. His book *Bharatiya Sanskriti* (Indian Culture) showed me his real self. It was a vision of not only Indian identity but of a world-view. He raised the slogan of 'Jai Jagat' (Hail Mother Earth) much before even Vinoba. When I read about his advocacy of family planning made in 1940-41, refusing to blindly endorse the views of Gandhi and Vinoba, I was dazzled by his scientific mind. The ideal prototypes of son, mother and wife were provided to me by his writings. When I talk to any foreigner about Guruji, they are shocked that such a great personality is not

known in other parts of the world. An ocean which managed to remain unrecognized due to his inborn humility can alone explain this phenomenon.

The influence that Sane Guruji had on the life of Baba has been eloquently eulogized in several of the latter's poems written originally in Marathi. Paying tribute to Sane Guruji, Baba writes in a poem titled 'The Tearful Log':

Because he cannot be everywhere
God created mother
And spread a canopy of affection.
Those feet whose families
Cannot fence in
For those struggling youngsters
He created
The mother-hearted superman
Sane Pandurang Sadashiv,
a loving guide of such struggling limbs.

Sane Guruji undertook a fast unto death to get the rights of the untouchables to enter the famous temple at Pandharpur. He remained dissuaded till the end despite Gandhi's efforts. Baba writes:

Your sainthood was not a garment nor a decoration
but the unfathomable humanity behind it
oozed from every word and dripped from every deed.
To free the imprisoned Almighty in Pandharpur
When you staked your life
Your butter-soft saintliness we saw becoming diamond-hard.
Lost in the heartbeats of your conscience, you
Refused to heed the object of your reverence,
your Mahatma.
Your arrogant humanity at that time
Was more scalding than the Devil's inferno and
more winsome than God's grace.

Shaken by the suicide of his philosopher, Baba questioned of him in pain:

They say
for a just man in an unjust world,
exist only two choices
prison and death.
Prison was no stranger to you
And death was sure to come some day
Why had you to invite it?
Piety, compassion, a prophet's vision you had
Why then did you become a defeated prophet?
You were alone, you were self-centre,
but were you also undemanding, devoid of attachment
Why then in non-hankering for life did you show
A yearning for death?

JESUS CHRIST

During his student days in Christian College, Baba resented attending Christian scripture classes. He did with ears plugged with cotton wool, because the classes were compulsory. But he read the Bible of his own accord, and via that, the life of Jesus Christ left a deep and longlasting impact on him: 'The cross is the emblem of crucifying one's life to make others happy. It makes us yield up the love of life for the life of love.'

Such was the impact of Christ's life on Baba that one of his friends called it the 'Christ syndrome'. 'I am a Hindu Brahmin, but I am also a follower of Christ.' It was under the influence of this 'Christ syndrome' that Baba saw Christ in all aspects, all forms of suffering, piety, sacrifice, compassion, love and life:

On the barbed wires rising from the black soil
on the smiling vines stretching out
seeing the bunches of grapes
raising his hand of benediction with blood oozing body,
I saw Christ...

Before I noticed a leper's wounds
I saw etched on his forehead
Your kiss of twenty centuries ago
And the body attaining perfection by that touch
Presented me the vision
of Michaelangelo's healthy humanity.
Your cross did not become an end of service
but a sign of all additions in life
did not signify persecution
but a declaration of piety.

But Baba prefers to be called a 'contemporary' of Christ rather than the 'disciple' of Christ. His understanding of Christ is that of Christ's essence, his foundation and not of walls of dogmas that have arisen in the course of history and hidden the true spirit of Christ. 'I am a follower of Christ, but not that sort of Christian who says, "I have an executive meeting at four thirty," while there is a man dying in the gutter.'

An inscription that stands on one of the main walls at the entrance to Anandwan reads:

I sought my soul but my soul I could not see
I sought my God but my God eluded me
I sought my brother and I found all three.

Michael Van Den Bogaert Sj, the director Xavier Institute of Management (Bubhaneshwar, Orissa) has said, 'I find this statement a fantastic summary of the challenge that faces all 'religious' persons of today in a society where there is much search for self and for God, but where organized religion is much misused for other purposes by our own Christian traditional structure and personnel included.' He also observes that, 'Without being a church member Baba Amte holds deep devotion to Lord Jesus. In Amte's model, community and manual work are clearly united as is the case with monastic orders in the Church.'

It is very evident from the beginnings of one of the many poems that Baba has written that it was the essence of Christ's teaching that attracted him and not Christianity as it was practised: 'Whenever Christianity is in conflict with "Churchianity", I squarely stand on the side of Christianity, because it is on this side that I have seen Jesus, who lends a helping hand to humanity, conquering forts.'

The saga of Jesus Christ and his equation with the sufferings of man was something that perennially inspired this sage from Anandwan. And this is the extent of the inspiration he gathered: 'The cross on which you spent your last breath has become to me not a sign that your service has come to an end. I see it as the sum of that which gives value to our life. To me it is not a symbol of violence wrought on you; to me it is the voice of compassion.'

According to Baba, Christ no longer bears the cross but a plough in the form of a cross, the plough representing an instrument that will create the agricultural progress of tomorrow. In the cross he sees the power that can change the hearts of men. It is a power that can transform the 'love of life' for the 'life of love' and thus prepare fields for the fulfilment of dreams of a happy tomorrow.

> I have seen a saddened Christ walking on a path on the edge of that devotion. He was not then carrying the cross on his shoulders, but the heavy burden of a plough in the shape of a cross. Deep peace shone from the eyes of him who carries the burden of the world, his face dripping with sweat.
>
> I immediately forsook the antiquated ways of devotion and began to walk in the footsteps of Christ, carrying the plough. The creative bearer of burdens, who walks in front of me, still continues on his way. I saw fearless workers digging the earth near the path of Christ, thus strengthening his way of life, and I saw on their sunburned backs rivulets of sweat carve a wet cross. I then had a vision of many Christs, and the assurance for a better future was mightily strengthened.

And finally in the most heartfelt and eloquent tribute that Baba could pay to the one whose words, actions and life provided him with immeasurable strength to devote his life to the service of humanity, he said, 'I haven't the arrogance to say that I can carry the mighty load of His cross, but I do try to walk in its shadow.'

It is clearly apparent then that besides great men, it was the Son of God, Jesus Christ, whose life of love and sacrifice was the source of emulation, appreciation and inspiration for Baba. Christ became the voice of his conscience and the emotion of his thoughts that drove him to action: 'When I prattle to my wife or young children, He says to me, "I have not seen your words in the company of deeds." To me Christ is the god sitting on my neck telling me, "You said this in the meeting but what have you done?" '

A poet that he is, Baba's words express his gratitude to all those forces that fuelled his motivation and fired his imagination:

Flying high in the sky and keeping my balance in the raging gale
and the strength of my wings
when I would feel
I had been catapulted
In the blind tornado
By such protective impulses
Of those impulses
Grateful awareness of loving assurance
Pacifies and arouses me even today,
those that shaped my meaningless existence
were the sun's allies.

slogan 'Break India', following that of Quit India. Baba was disturbed by a feeling that the vision of the country's bright future that he saw on the eve of independence along with many patriots would remain unfulfilled. This state of affairs in the nation was disturbing Baba's sensitive mind. He could see the country being ravished by pettiness, mean-mindedness and demons of social injustice, inequality, poverty, religion-based bigotry and such other prejudices. The only ray of hope he could see was the younger generation. He felt that the power of revitalizing the social structure to change the present picture of unhappiness, poverty, etc. lay with them. Whenever he got an opportunity to talk about the youth or with them, he emphasized the need to awaken and arouse them. In one of the messages to the youth he said, 'In these conditions if the youth wish to achieve something, they must break the shackles of passivity and caste differences.'

KNIT INDIA MOVEMENT

The turbulent happenings in the country during the late nineteen seventies and early nineteen eighties made every thinking citizen of India restless. While many would give in to the skepticism and cynicism about the role the citizens, high and low, play in national incidents and accidents, Baba would not take things lying down. He had two pillars of strength even in these distressing conditions – one was his dream of a strong and united India and the other was his unflinching faith that the youth can transform the nation once inspired. His belief was that 'the new leadership in India is taking shape quietly, without any drum beating, through the newspapers… maybe the surging new generation of today appears to have lost its bearings, to have lost its soul! But it is absolutely certain that one day it will have its own leader and prophet! This age will win over the destructive forces….' His intention of arousing the power of the youth is clearly indicated in his emotional speech before the volunteers who had come for the youth camp of Somnath. In his book *Ujwall Udyasahthi* (For a Bright Tomorrow) in Marathi, the text of his speeches allude to the underlying idea of 'Knit India' or 'Bharat Jodo' and the phrase itself has appeared in these speeches, 'The situation in the country is explosive. If the youth really want to do something, "Barat Jodo" is the real slogan, the real need.'

Finally in the November of 1984, the riots in Delhi and the whole of North India, as a sequel to the assassination of Mrs. Indira Gandhi, the then Prime Minister, compelled Baba to start the 'Knit India' campaign that was in its embryonic stage. In initiating and leading the campaign Baba was doing something that other greats had done before him and in which he had immense faith – the arousing of public concern through non-violent ways. There was Mahatma Gandhi's Salt March from Sabarmati to Dandi in 1930, Vinoba Bhave's seven year walk in the 1950s to persuade rich landowners to re-distribute their land in 1979. There was also the 5000km trans-Himalayan Chipko Walk led by Bahuguna to publicize the message of the Chipko Movement (this movement was dedicated to the protection and expansion of forests in India, in which the volunteers of the movement clung to trees in order to prevent their felling).

The assassination of Mrs. Indira Gandhi led to an unending chain of murders, internecine fights, bomb explosions, etc., and this fortified Baba's resolve to launch the 'Bharat Jodo' campaign. Baba felt that the conflicts between various castes, communities and linguistic groups, were growing. The conflicts had reached a point of explosion and in any other country such a state of affairs would have led to an armed revolt. The only solution to this pestering crisis was to understand each other in a spirit of togetherness. The UN declaration of the year 1985 as youth year, further strengthened Baba's determination. The idea that had obsessed him for many years, the desire to stop deterioration of the country on many fronts, manifested itself in the shape of the 'Bharat Jodo' or 'Knit India' campaign. Before launching the campaign, Baba wrote a letter to an eminent thinker and friend in which he explained his disturbed state of mind. In this letter Baba writes,

> Our country is suffering from various tensions! Envy, jealousy, caste conflicts, hidden economic, social and cultural fears have divided the society, as any right-thinking person can see. The minds of the youth are also bogged down with hopelessness, despair, frustration, as if it is the only common thread binding everyone together. This makes me ashamed of myself. I become immensely restless. I am keen to involve the youth in a campaign for national integration. Inactivity of the good persons results in strengthening of the evil. Therefore I have decided to march from Kanyakumari to Kashmir in the company of youth.

These were the circumstances leading to the beginning of the 'Knit India March' or 'Bharat Jodo Abhiyan'.

The pronouncement and planning of the Knit India campaign was finally made in the 'Shram Ashram Shibir' or the youth camp at Somnath in 1985. This march was to start from Kanyakumari on 24th December and travel 50–60km per day, to end at Jammu and Kashmir state after 107 days on 10th April, covering a distance of 5042km. Steps were taken to register the 'Bharat Jodo Samiti'. Enthusiastic calls, enquiries and applications started pouring in, which were then sorted out and the participants chosen. There were in all 116 participants chosen, including 16 women. The criteria for the selection, was simple and unbiased. The participants were to be in the age group of 21–35 years and were to be able to travel on a two-wheeler on varied road conditions, over a long distance. Those with ability to stage street plays, lead group songs, etc. were to be preferred. Participants were expected to lead a disciplined community life during the march. The organizers had expected to get at least three to four participants from each state. The group that was eventually formed had a preponderance of youth from southern and western India and only a sprinkling from the north and north-eastern regions. Only 12 days were allotted for complete rest during this bicycle tour of 5042km. Spread over 107 days demarcated in 95 phases with an average of 53km of travel per day! 24th December was chosen as the day for the commencement of this tour. This day was the birthday of Baba's mentor Sane Guruji, the day on which Swami Vivekananda gained his enlightenment and also the eve of the birth of Jesus Christ.

This campaign starting from Kanyakumari in southern India, in the International Youth Year on 24th December 1985 was to be terminated at Jammu-Kashmir state in the north on 9th April 1986 during the International Peace Year, thus giving it a special significance. Baba had said, 'It will now be desirable to imbibe aggressive peace. The peace which sits in a corner and sheds tears is no more of any use.'

The four-month-long cycle march would not have been possible without meticulous planning and organization. For this purpose, a 'Bharat Jodo Abhiyan' organizing committee was set up as the apex body for taking important decisions and management of men, materials and finances. Various local committees were also organized which were headed by Somnath youth campers, 'Antar Bharti' (a youth organization) workers, and many other people, who contributed in cash and kind and any other way they were called upon to. Each local committee sought mass response from the adjoining hamlets, villages, suburbs and towns, by mobilizing school and college teachers and students. They also undertook the task of collecting funds and resources, partly through the sale of 'Bharat Jodo' badges, stickers, diaries, T-shirts, posters and banners. The task of organizing public meetings and arranging for the lodgings of the participants on the way, also fell on the shoulders of these local committees.

Due to Baba's spinal injury he could not cycle, but that did not deter him as he decided to journey in a bus equipped with medical facilities. Siddharth Kak, an eminent TV personality, who was filming the whole campaign and had an opportunity to observe Baba closely, remembers,

> I wondered how he was going to manage his 'Bharat Jodo Yatra' from Kanyakumari to Kashmir, which we were filming, with a back condition like this. I needn't have worried. Baba would rise at four in the morning for his walk. We would be on the road by 6:30 a.m. Baba would travel lying down in his specially designed bus. On the way we would stop and Baba would address impromptu groups that had gathered to meet him. I witnessed the spontaneous affection of the people for the first time – the power generated by sainthood for a mass movement. In fact

> it was the first time I saw the 'real India', outside the cute tourist circuit.
>
> We were overwhelmed with hospitality on the road. At every halt we would be waved down and squash, cold drinks, fruits and snacks would be forced upon us and the hundred odd cyclists from all over India. There were girls too. We slept in schoolhouses or halls, ate wholesome vegetarian food prepared by volunteers, sitting cross-legged on the floor. We would attend meetings, sing songs, explore the cities and villages through which we passed. India unfolded before us in all its hues and contrasts, as our caravan rolled from the South to the North, relationships flowered, sundered, came together again. Slowly we became one large family. As we travelled we reached out to our own heritage and felt our roots stirring in our hearts. It was a 'Bharat Darshan' [tour of India] with a difference for all of us.

A typical day of the march started at 4 a.m. By 6 a.m. every participant was expected to complete his morning chores, pack up his belongings and load them into the accompanying truck. The march started exactly at 6 a.m. with a pilot jeep in the lead followed closely by the leader of the campaign, a young 27-year-old Atul Sharma, on a scooter, then a van modified into an ambulance for Baba was next. The tail was made up by the truck carrying the luggage. Moving at a speed of about 20–25km per hour, the march would continue till about 10–11 a.m. when the whole party would halt and call it a day. It was during these halts that people would gather from the neighbouring areas to see and hear Baba and also the songs, dance and dramas staged by the entourage.

Excerpts from some of the speeches rendered by Baba during the course of the march, and also pieces of thoughts expressed in various public meetings that were held, would themselves elucidate the aims that Baba hoped to achieve through this campaign:

> The fight against the British for independence was easier because you could see the enemy before you. The national integration movement is more complex since the enemy is invisible and is hiding within you and me.

For the nation's development, peace, cooperation and brotherhood are needed. The 'Bharat Jodo Campaign' has been designed to create them.

I became very restless seeing the lawlessness in the border states of Punjab and Assam and the bloodshed on the question of reservations. The idea of 'Bharat Jodo' was born against this background so as to appeal to the youth to carry the thought of national unity to the nooks and corners of the land. The burden of the new horizons cannot be carried by my generation's worn-out shoulders. I need the youth power for this task. I believe that in the modern world moving under the shadows of the guns, this generation alone can spread the message of fear-free peace and brotherhood.

The parliament can merely discuss the issue of national integration but cannot create the feeling of brotherhood and unity. The youth alone will have to shoulder this responsibility. The dream can only be fulfilled if the confidence that India can be knitted together is generated in every mind.

It is the misfortune of this generation that they have to witness the funeral pyre of their dreams. The 'Bharat Jodo' appeal has been made so that history does not have to record that India was further divided because the younger generation was not suitably warned.

I have raised the cry of 'Bharat Jodo' to save the generation tortured by casteism, sectarianism, and religious bigotry.

I have stayed at Anandwan amongst the deaf, dumb and disabled persons with weak bodies and strong minds. Today my mind weeps when I see around me strong bodies harbouring weak minds. Any seed can sprout in the soil, but in our hearts the seed of unity has failed to take root even after 36 years. This country had to witness the murder of another Gandhi. The community mind has been torn by the Hindu–Muslim conflict at the time of the first Gandhi murder and the Hindu–Sikh conflict at the time of the second. If this continues unabated, the future of the nation will become extremely bleak. Minds must be knitted together if the country is to be saved, and I have started marching with appeal of 'Bharat Jodo' with this aim.

> Today I have reached the land of Lord Rama. The Lord Rama of the youth of today is much stronger, but he has lost his arrow of sensitivity. In search of this arrow, I am marching with this mini-India.
>
> Today the youth is not working in the right direction even though the national borders have been the crater of a volcano and several urgent problems facing the nation defy solution. So, to warn the youth and not merely to appeal to them that the right time for action is now, not later, I have set out on the 'Bharat Jodo' pilgrimage.
>
> In this land of martyrs having a rich heritage and culture, the younger generation appears to be tending towards self-indulgence rather than altruism. The generation does not explode at the sight of inequality. To awaken the younger generation, I am making a pilgrimage of the country in the company of the youth.
>
> I have started the 'Bharat Jodo' march to create a band of youth who love their country.
>
> A question that vexes my mind is, 'Has the younger generation compromised its conscience? Do the words in the books (scriptures) fail to communicate with them?' I hope that the vision that will possess the youth will communicate with them, help them get over their paralysis. This is an attempt to arouse the pulse of the youth and their spirit for rebuilding our nation.

These aims and ambitions with which Baba set out in the company of his 'band of youth', he disbursed through his words amongst the people of villages, towns and cities, whom he encountered along the way. His haste in moving and meeting as many of his countrymen as he could, arose from his realization that time was not on his side, it was slipping away fast, and he still had to do much. His way with words was the instrument he used in order to break the stupor of inactivity of the youth, and it worked. And finally he sealed the aim behind the march, with a solemn pledge that became a morale booster for the participants of the campaign, in the face of the difficulties they faced during the march:

I believe a great aim leads to great sacrifice. I will reach deep into my heart and soul and say that I will move a little from the comfort of my life to understand the hurt of the hungry and the oppressed.

I pledge I will have more concern for others than control of others.

I give an assurance that I am eager to do social service not for self-glory but for the glory of my nation.

I believe that words can never take the place of action.

I will be strong and noble in my aspirations. I will be long on deeds and short on words.

I pledge I will add to the nation's happiness, the learning and the liberties of mankind.

I am convinced that love costs nothing but pays a lot.

Lofty thoughts are sweet; lofty action is sweeter. Selfless action is the soul of social service.

I seek neither pleasure nor name but the fellowship of pain.

I pledge I will live and die for the union of the souls.

I believe that a free and fearless mind can work wonders. He is rich whose life is enriched by action.

PEACE BY PEACE MISSIONS

A whole year had elapsed since the assassination of Prime Minister Indira Gandhi by her Sikh bodyguards, but what erupted in the wake of this assassination were still as aggressively defiant, menacing and hideous as they had been then. The heartless massacre of the Sikhs in North India had turned Punjab into a veritable bomb, in retaliation. The state of 'the five rivers' was hurt, discontented and disturbed. And with every passing day the situation deteriorated further. The government's best efforts failed in containing the surge of anger and hatred, which kept churning out militants. No solution seemed to be the right one. The leaders, politicians and intellectuals, all of them had no options, no answers, no ways out of this effervescent situation. The disgruntled lot in Punjab was making a very strong emotional appeal by passing of the 'Anandpursahib Resolution', to show the rest of the world that the entire Sikh community was behind the proposal of the creation of an independent nation and to bring the entire Sikh community, and especially the Sikh youth, behind the independent 'Khalistan' movement. The leader of the 'Khalistan' (pure country) movement Bhindrawale and his followers had garnered support from Sikhs living overseas and were engaged in extremist talk of separation, voicing the aim of an independent Sikh nation. The centuries-old friendship and goodwill amongst the Sikh and Hindu communities was being breached.

The state of Punjab was thus extremely volatile when Baba first visited it during the 'Bharat Jodo' march. This visit lasted eight days, during which Baba met and conferred with many people at Chandigarh, Hoshiarpur, Batala, Jalandhar and Anandpursahib, so that he could get a true picture of the happenings at various places in the state. He also met the disillusioned, the restless and the frightened and also those who were seeking support, sympathy and assurance and even the disgruntled and vindictive. He was meeting all these people as an ordinary citizen since he was of the view that it was not a problem of the people and government of Punjab alone but of every citizen of the country. He was unafraid of the militants and their militancy, 'One who takes his life into his hands recognizes and respects another similar soul,' and with this conviction he visited the most tense areas and even the extremist camps! One of the participants of the march recalls, 'Baba warned bluntly. "Under no circumstances will the march stop. Even if there is firing and one of you falls, the rest will march ahead. The doctors will look after the injured. Even if I were to die, the campaign will proceed to Jammu and reach there exactly on schedule."'

The Commissioner of the Municipal Corporation on behalf of the citizens of Amritsar extended a warm welcome to Baba and said in his address:

> Today your slogan *'Jaat bhed ke bandhan todo, Bharat Jodo, Bharat Jodo'* [break the shackles of caste and creed and unite India] is resounding throughout the length and breath of the country. It gives us great pleasure to welcome you, along with your band of youthful workers on this soil. At this age, braving all hazards and vagaries of

> weather, you have arrived here to inspire us with your feelings of love and humanism. We, the citizens of Amritsar, need barely assure you that we are deeply beholden to and your companions for reminding us of our obligations to our motherland and to our fellow brethren. We shall cherish the sweet memory of your visit for a long time to come. Let us all pray that your message continues to inspire us all.

After Baba's first visit to the strife-torn Punjab, no one conjectured that he would go back there where others did not dare to even look. He said 'My critic friends thought that "Bharat Jodo" got publicity and became a hot topic for discussion and that was the end of it. Why would I go again to Punjab? Even the people did not expect me to go back there, and that too so soon. A leading daily of Punjab wrote, "Bharat Jodo Yatra came like a storm and went off like a tornado. What next?" However I went there as per predetermined programme.'

The second visit to Punjab took place from 1st July 1986 to 9th August 1986. At a time when the police had become helpless and ineffective in stopping terrorist activities, political leaders had been rendered more or less irrelevant, and the future of Punjab looked as depressing as never before, Baba along with his eight-member team left for the troubled land. In the first phase of this visit 35 places were visited, and 15 more were visited in the second phase. In all they covered 50 villages and contacted members of 85 families, scouring even the most sensitive and violent areas. They held talks with editors, journalists, intellectuals, trade union leaders, politicians, doctors, professors and other important local citizens in the major cities. They also included in their assignment, sharing of the pain of the bereaved families, consoling them, reaffirming their hope and faith in humanity. In the interval between the first two visits, Baba made two trips to Delhi to apprise the Prime Minister of the gravity of the Punjab situation. But he had to face disappointment. The PM felt no urgency about the problem and showed little involvement. He believed that the deployment of the army would take care of the situation, whereas Baba felt that the deployment of the army was not the solution, and it would have adverse repercussions.

Conditions in Punjab were deteriorating rapidly and none of the leaders seemed ruffled by it in the least. It was the second death anniversary of the assassination of Indira Gandhi, and in Amritsar in the Golden Temple complex posters paying tribute to the 'martyrs' of the Khalistan movement and also those assuring the formation of a new nation were being displayed. So Baba decided to visit Punjab for the third time on 25th September 1986. Before leaving he wrote a letter to the then President Sh. Venkatraman:

Dear Rashtrapati Venkatramanji,

I am leaving for Punjab to carry out my mission of Peace by Peace. Even now the tools of bilateral diplomacy and mutual understanding can be readily summoned in the cause of peace in Punjab.

The mutual understanding between the two communities – whether Sikh and Hindu or Hindu and Muslim – should be national agenda no: 1. History dictates to us.

We must act now; otherwise it will take another generation of leaders to acknowledge that the two communities must build a common future because they share a common past.

I am affluent in affection and am carrying with me a tightly packed bundle of confidence and the delicious burden of gratitude about our countrymen. I will keep my tears of gratitude in my memory while I walk in Punjab – the Lonely Mission of Love. The master of infinite compassion – Gandhiji – is guiding my trembling feet. He is a light upon my path. What has been happening in Punjab is a storm signal. It is time I bid farewell to my weaknesses and lean on His strength.

The dedicated team of my close associates from Kerala, Karnataka, Maharashtra, Gujarat, Delhi, belonging to different communities viz. Christian, Hindu, Sikh, are accompanying me on this risky but challenging mission. I have tremendous faith in the youth fascinated by broad shouldered purposes, motivated to restore amity among the children of Mother India.

I seek your goodwill in my endeavour to wipe the tears of the grief-stricken citizens of Punjab.

With kind regards,
Yours sincerely,
Sd/-
Baba Amte.

This time he visited all the border outposts. During the stay of Baba and his team in the Gurudwaras located in the so-called terrorist-infested areas, they were treated in a very civil manner but with no enthusiasm for discussions. At other places Baba was sometimes called names, shouted at and accused of insincerity, by angry groups and individuals. One of the team members has recorded, 'Every day was frustrating. We had expected to hold talks, meetings, discussions, with the disgruntled elements to bring them to the point of compromise and consensus. But nothing came about. Baba used to be very sad and unhappy at the end of the day. He would express his dissatisfaction at the state of affairs. But the next morning he was back with added vigour, faith and enthusiasm. He enthused us all with faith every morning. It was like a pendulum, swinging from depression in the evening to ardent zeal the next morning.'

The main aim of these visits, according to Baba, was, 'We visited the tense areas and gave courage to Hindus and Sikhs, tried to mollify them. Like the 'Hit List' of the extremists, we had a 'Hamdardi List' (Empathy list). Baba has described his Peace by Peace mission as his life's last and lasting mission.

During his Knit India movement from Kanyakumari to Jammu and Kashmir and the Peace by Peace missions to Punjab, Baba realized there were numerous problems in independent India which were silently becoming violent and disruptive day by day. So he decided to venture out on the roads once more, this time he planned to march from east to west of India in an attempt to review and revive situations in these areas by direct contact with the people. He desired for the youth to know better the seven neglected states in the North-East of the country. So little is known about them that most people are not able to tell the names of their capitals easily as well as the names of the rivers flowing through them. The movement for independence had hardly touched these states, and even after independence this part remained neglected. Baba wanted the youth to see for themselves the reason for the neglect of this part of the country and try to find some solutions for it. With this aim in view began the second 'Bharat Jodo' march on 1st November 1987 which was to cover a distance of 7,546km during a period of 146 days, culminating on 26th March, 1988. It would start from Itanagar in the east and end at Okhla in the west. And like during the first march, in the second one too the people welcomed the participants warmly, listening carefully to the message of national integration that they were carrying.

Assessing the missions and marches undertaken by Baba in terms of successes and failures would be trivializing the intention behind them. And when the intention is love, it is bound to touch the hearts of the people, the effect of which is not visible on political and economic graphs of a nation. It is as essential to move the hearts of men as it is to motivate their minds and this aim is achievable only by going out and reaching them. Someone had to go out there to soften the hearts of people with love so that their minds could then work out solutions to various problems, and Baba took it upon himself to be that someone.

> Repeatedly in history, the petty machinations of small calculating men, the brokers of power, have tried to pit one section of our people against the other, by sowing the poison of hatred in their minds. Sadly, for a while many of us have fallen prey, drawn to this frenzy of communal passion. What follows is never the gain of any community....
>
> —Baba speaking through the press.

CHAPTER 12

The Final Act: The Narmada Beckons

> Around eighty of us met at Anandwan, at Warora, in the first week of July 1988 to express our grave concern about the devastation caused by big dams. We came from different parts of the country all united in a common resolve – to ensure that people were no longer denied their basic rights over natural resources. We affirmed that the nation's rivers are the cradle of our civilization and that they cannot be strangulated to meet the needs of the exploiting class within society.
>
> The issues raised by the construction of big dams challenge the very concept of the present pattern of economic growth, unquestioningly adopted by our planners. Nothing less than the survival of the life itself is at stake for very many of our people and time is running out rapidly. We appeal to the nation to halt all big dams here and now.
>
> The Anandwan Declaration on the construction of the Narmada Dams.

Anandwan organized and sponsored a national conference attended by approximately 80 esteemed and renowned environmentalists and scientists. In this conference was drafted and adopted the 'Anandwan Declaration', which vehemently opposed the construction of big dams in India, giving reasons of their opposition of such projects and suggesting alternatives for them as well. They also organized an internationally televised protest of 30,000 people at the village of Harsud, one out of a hundred villages that would be sunk if the construction of the Narmada dams were to be completed.

In 1988 Baba became the first Asian to win the United Nation's Human Rights Award, taking a place in history alongside Robert F. Kennedy and Martin Luther King Jr.

Somewhere in early 1990s Baba made a public announcement, saying that he had decided to leave Anandwan forever. 'We were stunned,' says Prakash, 'he had not spoken a word about it to us. Not even to mother. He knew we would never give our consent in this matter, in view of his health, so he announced it in front of hundreds of people and left us with no option but to let him go.' He was 77 years old, two pacemakers managed his heart, eye-drops his cataract condition, nearly two dozen pills numerous other ailments, and a brace and wooden staff his cervical spondylosis, besides this Tai's concoction of basil, turmeric and milk. 'She thinks it will make me fair,' chuckles Baba with a mischievous twinkle. But 'Mayia Rewa' (River Narmada) and millions of her tribal sons were in distress. The government was intent on pursuing its monstrosity of impounding the mighty river in gigantic dams that were threatening to lap up the lives and lands of the innocent unaware farmers and tribals. Pain has great power over Baba. 'God, give us pain,' he says, 'so that we could feel tenderness.' And God gave him so immense a pain for the hapless tribals that he decided to go and live amongst them for the rest of his days and fight with his ebbing energies to restore their rights through 'aggressive militant peace'.

'The moment has come for me to leave Anandwan, the place where I made my beginning into the world of joy; the place that symbolizes the very meaning of my existence. I am leaving to live along the Narmada, to remain in communion with her, to attain a peace that all mankind desires.'

Just as Baba was planning to leave Anandwan forever, he received a letter from the Templeton Foundation, headquartered in Nassau in the Bahamas, apprising him that he had been selected as an awardee of the Templeton Prize for Progress in Religion. Baba wrote back that he was immensely obliged for the honour bestowed upon him but expressed his inability to receive the award himself, firstly due the condition of his spine, and besides he was locked in a battle over the Narmada dams.

As always Baba pursued whatever he took up with so fierce a passion that it consumed all else without remorse or guilt. On 6th March 1990, bold headlines flashed across a number of national and international dailies confirming the departure of Baba to Choti Kasarvad, a small headland overlooking the waters of the Narmada. 'Baba Amte's Vanaprastha', is how Rajni Bakshi has referred to this phase of Baba's life in her book *Bapu Kuti: Journeys in the Rediscovery of Gandhi.* All appeals and criticisms failed to dampen his determination, 'Many people, even my sons, feel I am wasting my life on the Narmada.... I have cured the leprosy of the body. Now I have to cure the leprosy of the mind.'

The saga of the Narmada was set in the mid nineteen eighties. It meandered through three decades and three States of the Indian Union carrying in its waters the mire of a terrible conflict; the conflict between the compulsions of producing power for industry and the need to protect the environment and the basic rights of the people. This complex saga of thirty years is so inextricably enmeshed in dharnas (sit-ins), Satygraghas (non-violent protests), fasts, slogans and marches by the opponents of the issue and court rulings, arrests and plans and policies of the proponents of the issue, that to disentangle it would be no mean feat. However, the basic plot gives a fairly sufficient and clear picture of the story. The Narmada belts around India from east to west. Emerging from the Maikal ranges at Amarkantak in Madhya Pradesh in the east, it girdles around a 1300km stretch of mountains, gorges and alluvial patches. This journey of one of the seven most sacred rivers of India, through the three states of Madhya Pradesh, Maharashtra and Gujarat, sees culmination when its waters drain into the Arabian Sea. For centuries this mighty river has been the benevolent benefactor giving millions livelihood and homes on its banks and making the landscape picturesque. It defines everything from the landscape to the lives of men in the three states through which it flows. It has an uncanny living, breathing presence, with people ardently loving, worshipping and protecting it. And then one day the government puts out an unfair, unjust plan that disturbs the peaceful co-existence of the men and their river; the plan was to corral Goddess Narmada into a series of huge stepped reservoirs. It was decided that in all 30 large dams, 135 medium and 3000 small dams were to be built in order to harness the waters of the Narmada and its tributaries. However, the Sardar Sarovar dam was to be the largest of these dams, with a proposed height of 136.5 metres (445 feet!), and it became the focal point of both the dam builders and opposers of the dam. The building of this dam meant the displacement of 320,000 people and the deprival of the livelihood of a thousand others. It also meant the submergence of thousands of hectares of agricultural and forest land. The total displacement of people by the time of completion of the whole canal system is estimated to be one million! If all the dams are to be built, the river will disappear leaving behind only a series of lakes as its reminders. The tribals and farmers, though all aghast and angered, had no way of fighting against the players of politics. And so the construction of the dams started, heedless of the cultural annihilation of the peoples whose homes began to be swallowed up by the flooding waters of the demon dams. A few hundreds of these oustees were 'generously' relocated by the government on barren, dry patches while a thousand others were left to perish as punishment for not cooperating with the government in drowning their homes!

It is here amongst these people rendered homeless that Baba comes to live. As always Baba's home is an unpretentious thatched hut in the close vicinity of an ancient Shiva Temple with the Narmada flowing around in complete serenity, brilliance, placidity and abundance. He visits the Shiva temple along with Tai and even rings the huge brass bell of the temple for her. It is not a change of heart, not a crossover from being spiritual to religious, he does it merely because 'it makes her happy!' he says with affection. 'He began to see his own existence with the quietude of "Rewa Mayia" [Mother Narmada] as a manifestation of what he calls a "Post- revolution Perspective".' At just about the time that Baba moved to Kasarvad, the pulling down of the Berlin Wall had signalled the collapse of communism. This event marked a turning point in the history of ideas. Perhaps now Baba thought, the world would be ready to accept what he had learnt in his youth from Gandhiji and Tagore – that every revolution devours its children:

> There is a danger that tomorrow's blade of the guillotine may be smeared with your blood.... A true revolution is not destructive but creative. Its face is not smeared with blood but covered with sweat. Negative slogans may appear at first more powerful, but they are short-lived, constructive movements, though they may appear weak, have a touch of lastingness.
>
> From Rajni Bakshi's *Bapu Kuti: Journeys in the Rediscovery of Gandhi*

Here at Kasarvad he lies on his bed in sun and shade. A burgeoning grove has sprung up around the cottage built on the banks of the Narmada by the locals near the village of Badwani, as the illegal site of his protest against the building of the dam. Here with the Rewa Mayia in full view he lies musing, 'This is the place where I could build a dialogue with myself and detect the minutest vibrations of my mother, Narmada. We should decorate her with small dams that don't interfere with her flow,' he said. In his Templeton Prize acceptance speech, which was read out by Vikas at the Buckingham Palace, he brings the Narmada issue to the notice of the world at large:

> I am assaulted by the insensitivity and aggression of those who wish to build atomic reactors, polluting factories and large dams. They think nothing of the living resources they kill. They think nothing of men, women and children who depend on these resources for their existence. Their immorality has assumed astounding proportions. Today I have become part of the battle to save the Narmada, one of the most sacred rivers of the Indian tradition. The battle is not to save the Narmada alone. The larger goal is to bring the message of Mother Earth to the whole world. To stop the process of destructive development and to bring in this new vision – of a new way of being in the world.

There are various fronts of disagreements between the government and the members of the NBA–Narmada Bachao Andolan (Save the Narmada Campaign), headed by the dynamic Medha Patkar. Baba's entire support and sympathy lies with Medha and the NBA, and so he becomes their most vociferous voice, without actually becoming a member of their campaign. There are a number of points of dissension that he has with the construction of the giant dams on the Narmada. The Sardar Sarovar Project (SSP) has been hailed as the lifeline of Gujarat, as the permanent solution to the water problem of Suarashtra and Kutch, as the panacea for Gujarat's drought-prone, arid and tribal acres. Sadly, each of these claims is a blatant lie. Careful examination of the government's own disaggregated data shows that 56 out of 69 talukas of water-starved Saurashtra (i.e. 81%) are to get no water from the SSP. Two thirds of Gujarat's drought-prone or arid talukas are to get little or no water from the project. 42 out of 47 tribal talukas and pockets are also not to receive a drop of water from the SSP.

As for the Narmada Sagar Project (NSP) in Madhya Pradesh, its main rationale is storage of water for the SSP. The extent of irrigation it is to provide for the people of M.P. is, believe it or not, less than the area to be submerged in M.P. by NSP and SSP. No wonder then that the people of the Narmada valley are up in arms against these people. The people of Gujarat must also wake up to the terrible financial burden the SSP is going to prove to them. Baba said:

> Finally and above all I oppose the NSP and SSP for the large scale cultural ethnocide they will perpetrate. I refer to the three lakh people living in the submergence zones who will be rendered homeless by the two projects. Already more than 50,000 people living in the submergence zones of the Tawa and Bargi projects of the Narmada have had to flee with nowhere to go. The people of the Narmada valley, with their long experience of talks with officials spread over many years at every level, have come to the conclusion that just and developmental re-settlement is impossible, whatever be the claims, promises and paper-policies of the government.

According to the *New Internationalist* (July 2001 issue):

> Since 1950, at least 25 million people in India have been displaced by large projects. Of these 40% are Adivasis or tribals, who constitute only 8% of India's population. It is the predicament of indigenous people everywhere. Who says you own the forest? Where are your title deeds? Over time they have been increasingly hemmed in to remote corners and designated 'encroachers' of their own lands. The statistics say that 50% of those displaced by large projects have been pauperized. In the lands beyond Bargi Nagar, the proportion is closer to 100%. These include farmers as well as craftsmen and merchants. A few people starved to death or died of hopelessness in the terrible years between 1990 and 1993 when the state literally drowned them. Most are now real paupers or have ended as the cheapest of labour, pulling rickshaws in Jabalpur. Self-sufficient farmers who once had self-respect have become lowly servants of others, grateful for the job of a watchman.

Of a total of 3600 big dams, 3300 have been built after independence. Yet one fifth of the population has no drinking water and two thirds lack even basic sanitation. Over 90 crores have been spent on irrigation, and ironically drought still persists relentlessly in the country.

Despite his 77 years Baba was still the man of action we have known him to be so far. In March 1990, he came to live on the ghats (banks) of the Narmada carrying with him an unjust share of illnesses. But could they deter him? On the Christmas day of 1990, Baba, Medha and more than 6000 farmers and tribals embarked on an epic 200km March from Madhya Pradesh to the dam site in Gujarat, with the aim of drawing national and international attention to human right abuses. This formidable human chain was, however, unceremoniously brought to a halt at the Gujarat border by a large guard of armed police. All of Baba's appeals to the authorities, to be allowed to complete this peaceful demonstration, were turned down. The protestors began getting agitated and forcing themselves through the police barricade, many of them were arrested, and the rest had to terminate the march. The Sardar Sarovar is rising up. The plan is to drown 1.27 lakh hectares of fertile agricultural land and natural forest with this dam and another, the SSP, in order to irrigate 1.8 hectares of land. An additional 0.8 hectares of land will be taken over in building all the irrigation channels, and the land that will be needed for project colonies, power houses, new roads and quarries is not even calculated here! But Baba is not going to give up. He is determined to make the government see its foolishness and save the river valley people, even if he is drowned by the precariously rising waters. The people are with him and together they form what Baba calls the 'drown and die' squad. 'I ask not to know, I ask not to see, I ask to be completely used in this work before I walk in the silent company of the nature God.' But on 6th December 1992, the country faced another terrible debacle – the demolition of the Babri Masjid at Ayodhya by Hindu extremists. There was an outbreak of riots in many parts of India and people were gripped with panic and terror. Gory reports from all over unravelled terrible tales of how thousands of innocent lives were being savagely extinguished. Baba once again could not shut out the cries of so much pain. He could not fight his desire to be with the people despite his physical disabilities. In an appeal to the nation, just before he and Tai set out for the riot-torn Mumbai, he made an appeal to the nation:

> I am setting out on what God may deem to be the last and most important pilgrimage of my life, a journey into the hearts and minds of the people of India. The blinding haze of dust raised by the demolition of a mosque in Ayodhya forces me to break my self-imposed exile on the banks of the Narmada. Today at the age of 79, I pray to God that my disobedient, broken body obey the compelling dictates of my conscience. I came here, leaving my whole life behind to build, together with the Adivasis of the Narmada Valley, a new indigenous vision of compassionate, sustainable development. My opposition to the construction of large destructible dams on the Narmada will remain to my last breath. But today I must set out to dam the enormous river of tears that the devastation in and after Ayodhya has unleashed.
>
> The catastrophe that looms ahead is not just the balkanization of

the country – what is threatened is the balkanization of the hearts and minds of our people. It is as if, the soul of the nation has died. All that we cherished and lived by, the unassailable spirit of oneness that invigorated you, that carried this nation through the sternest of challenges, has been delivered a death-blow. This spirit has to be rebuilt, renewed, revived. Today I want to ask each one of you – can anything large and beautiful, sacred and enduring be built on the foundation of humiliation and suspicion, vengeance and destruction? Is it right for us to make the weak and innocent pay today for what we consider to be the mistakes of history? And where will this barbarism lead, when will this vandalism end? How many Masjids will be razed to the ground, how many Mandirs will be destroyed before our hate finds satiation?

What we are witness to today is the absolute perversion of the sacred teachings of our tradition. As the Bhagwad Gita says, God resides in the heart of every being. All religions of the world speak of the omnipresence of God and the oneness of all God's creations. This oneness is also the real insight of modern science and our renewed environmental consciousness. God can never be restricted to just one spot, nor can we insist on just one path to God's realization. The different faiths are only different ways of approaching and realizing the oneness of God. Through the flowering of these many blossoms, the garden of God only becomes all the more fragrant.

An enormous challenge beckons all those who take pride in this glorious tradition of Indian civilization. Let us come together to remove every trace of hatred from the hearts of our people, let us say a firm and unyielding 'NO' to those who try to divide us in the name of religion, let us resolve never to be part of this cycle of retribution and revenge. Let us build at the disputed site at Ayodhya neither Mandir nor Masjid, but a true temple of love, our own gift to the children orphaned in this mad violence, a place where they could receive tender care and wholesome upbringing. Let Ayodhya become a symbol of human brotherhood and unity of tolerance and love, of the oneness of the spirit, which is the true essence of all religions.

Let each of us perform at least one act of atonement for what has been debased in our humanity itself, and it must, therefore, be atoned for by each and every one of us. We owe this act of reparation above all, to our future generations, our children, who will otherwise never forgive our complicity in these heinous crimes, which are nothing less than harbingers of fascism, never seen before in our land.

Wherever we live, especially in every village, street or locality, where violence has taken place, let us form Peace and Unity Committees, comprising members of all communities. Let each member develop personal contact with the victims of violence, preferably belonging to a different community, and do everything possible for their relief and rehabilitation and to restore a sense of security and hope among them. Let us jointly rebuild all property destroyed in the violence,through collective 'Shram Dan' by members of all communities. Let us also reach out to the hearts and minds of those who have succumbed to this madness and bring back to them the real meaning of religion and humanity. Let us strain our every nerve to rebuild a feeling of unity within these fractured neighbourhoods.

For the moment, let us set aside everything else that may seem pressing or important, let us bury all our differences. Mother India beckons us all. Let the cry go around in every nook and corner of this great land.

From '*Ek dooje ki nafrat chhodo, Bharat Jodo, Bharat Jodo*!'
(Stop the hatred for each other, unite India)

At Mumbai, where men were being mercilessly butchered, Baba and Tai stayed on for a month. Speaking through the press, Baba appealed to almost everyone to stop the human carnage in the name of religion. When he returned to Kasarvad, he was a man visibly swamped with sadness.

The year is 1993 and August 6th has been fixed as the day for the 'Jal Samadhi'. Baba says that the government has till August 5th to decide, and if it does nothing, then Baba, Medha and thousands of tribals would not leave their huts and drown themselves in the waters of the dam that are rising rapidly. 'If our lives are what will take them to realize their error, we are ready for that. At least we will be able to save those that will live on after we are gone.' But Baba and Tai, his loyal life-mate, were forcibly evacuated to the circuit house in Badwani by the police when the waters reached the doorstep of their humble abode, as if coming to claim them. In 1994, Medha and a few others went on a hunger strike. When the strike entered the 20th day and the condition of the strikers became critical, Baba demanded vehemently of the government to stop the construction of the dam and warned that if anything was to happen to any of the NBA activists, especially Medha, the situation would become explosive.

Although the Narmada had come on the international stage way back in 1988, the World Bank went ahead with its agenda of funding the project. 'The damaging effects of destructive development would also be aired on an international level to bring pressure on funding agencies like the World Bank, asserted the Anandwan Declaration way back in 1988. But the threat of this assertion was now actually being felt. As conditions began getting volatile in India, under immense international pressure the World Bank cancelled its $450 million loan in 1993. However the state government rushed in to fill the gap and the construction of the dam was kept going. It is only in 1995 that the Supreme Court ordered halting of the construction but only after the dam had already reached a height of 80.3 metres. Is the battle won? Baba is not too trusting of the government, which is given to making and breaking promises at will.

> As a nation today, we face a crisis of faith and credibility. Moving to the remote tribal regions, the bonds grow more tenuous and fragile. Each one of us has to reach out, to intimately experience the sorrows and tribulations of peoples and cultures who feel increasingly marginalized and threatened with extinction. I look to our young to provide the energy and the healing touch – a touch suffused with creativity and imagination for building anew from the earth.
>
> The Indian village, like a woman, carries the entire nation in her womb. For a healthy nation to develop she needs careful nurturing. Becoming one with our village people, we must give back what we have taken away from them – their self-confidence and their control over their own destiny.
>
> When the trainee becomes the trainer, hands become eloquent. Eloquent hands refuse to carry a beggar's bowl. Eloquent hands not

only build homes and factories, they also build a nation, a culture, a people.

We haste on heedless forgetting the flowers on the roadside hedge
Yet they breathe, unaware of our forgetfulness, filling it with music.

The grudge of Baba and his team of opposers against the damming of the Narmada was very basic, and alternatives to big dams were suggested and drafted in the 'Anandwan Declaration': 'There was not a single example of a large dam constructed in India, which could be held out as a model for development. Not one dam had delivered as it had promised. Every dam had destroyed more property than it claimed it would, without satisfactorily rehabilitating those ousted from it.' Also the opposers felt that the argument of the government that large dams offered inevitable solutions to the flood situation in the country. It had not a single iota of truth in it. They asserted that after the construction of over 1500 large dams, the flood situation has not gone even close to the promised improvement. It was further pointed out in the Declaration that 'small dams, reservoirs, percolation tanks, bunds, check dams, etc. could easily solve the water problems of our people as they provide employment to millions. Mini green belts could be created around these small water bodies, thus providing shade and fodder, raising the water table and protecting the soil over vast areas. This step, along with appropriate agricultural techniques such as dry farming and drip irrigation, can transform India. As for the requirements of power, instead of planning new big dams, we should be concentrating on improving the conditions of our existing white elephants. Every dam will live out its usefulness earlier than anticipated because of siltation.' It was agreed in the Anandwan resolution later that, 'a national consensus on alternatives to large dams should be sought. India is a country where the rain falls fast and furious for a few short months. The rainwater should be caught and held where it falls. This can be the only long term, sustainable alternative to large dams.' Besides, Baba also has suggested that if the government really had the development of the country in mind, it should promote inexpensive technologies like methane digesters, improved low-fuel cook-stoves, solar heating and rainwater catchments in the villages. 'I'm not against dams. I'm against big dams. We must attempt to answer the critical question – what is the level of maximum permissible submergence, in terms of people, forests and agricultural land? In determining the size of any river valley project, we must regard this as the decisive criterion. No project which exceeds this level of submergence should be granted clearance.' The benefits of these large dams get siphoned off to distant urban centres over the death and destruction of the lives of the rural and tribal lot. Good planning includes sufficiency for all before excess for a few. The success of Baba's farming and small-scale water hoarding techniques in Anandwan and other projects is sound evidence that there is a far more cost-effective and much less disruptive alternative to big dams. Big dams have never been known to irrigate as much land as they promise and provide the least benefit to those whose need is the largest. 'What kind of world is this that you need millions of gallons of water to fill your swimming pool, to wash your car, to make chemicals that will pollute the water remains, when so many millions cannot even find water to wet their lips?' Baba is flabbergasted by the injustice being perpetrated in the name of senseless development.

> The worldwide environmental movement contains the glimmers of a new hope. To realize this hope, however, it must concentrate on the essentials and discard the fads. The essential, the eternal, the sustainable living. Living which restrains desire, which respects the diversity of life – plant, animal and human. Living which is founded on compassion – that seeks the creation of a world in which there is sufficiency for all before there is superfluity for some.
>
> It is really so straightforward. Look at the honeybee. It's treasure of nectar, obtained from a plant of chillies, is not at the cost of the flower. In fact, it's the act of extracting honey that delivers development and progress to the flowers. Can the same be said of our modes of development and intervention?
>
> —From Baba's Templeton Prize acceptance speech

Due to the efforts of Baba and the NBA the construction of the Sardar Sarovar Project remained discontinued from 1994 to 1999. However in 1999 the Supreme Court of India passed its ruling in the case; it gave the go-ahead for the height of the SSP to be raised to 88 metres. And despite the best efforts of all concerned, in 2000, the Supreme Court authorized construction up to the originally planned height of 138 metres. The nation was stunned and the woes of Medha Patkar were to continue. Almost two decades ago, a young, energetic and vibrant Medha of 35 years, started out with full gusto in her drive to oppose the construction of the SSP. She sought support and guidance from Baba who had already begun his own campaign against the river valley project, even though some activists of the NBA felt that Baba's sheer stature would swerve the focus of the issue. And Baba in turn threw his entire might behind the cause Medha had undertaken. For a while it seemed that the efforts of these two passionate souls had come to nought. But these are people made of rare alloys – while Medha still continues her struggle even today with the same fervour, Baba feels as strongly of the issue as ever. However, Baba had to return to Anandwan in the mid-year of 2001 owing to Tai's illness and entreaties of friends and family to return. All kinds of conjectures were afloat on his return; specially on the part of the government, which sensed a whiff of victory in Baba's removal of himself from the scene of protest as the presence of so lofty a personality as Baba, protesting at Kasarwad, had all along proved the biggest impediment in their schemes of carrying out the construction of the dams. The spokespersons of the government leapt at the opportunity and began issuing sensational reasons for Baba's return to Anandwan:

> Excellent success of the state's rehabilitation work among the dam oustees. This should have taken place earlier. The NBA sponsored anti-development thinking cannot last long. It is good that Baba Amte has understood this now. If he had undertaken this step earlier, he would have been regarded as great fighter against leprosy in the ashram among the adivasis, as also a server of the people who suffered from drought.

Definite information that serious differences have arisen between the NBA and him over the issue of the rehabilitation of the oustees. He has been feeling neglected and cheated.

The NBA publicly denied these allegations stating the illness of Tai as Baba's sole reason for his return, and Baba's sons Vikas and Prakash confirmed this. Prakash says, 'For the first time our mother asked Baba to do something for her. She was sick and lonely without him and also worried about his health as he had been living for ten years now in Kasarwad, and the living conditions were harsh. So she almost forced him to return saying that it would be the first and last time she would ever ask anything of him. He had to return.' Baba doesn't say much even on being prodded, only this, 'I had to do this for her.' But his heart is still with the people who are drowning and perishing and so his poetic musings continue:

> Shall I take a knife and tear my mother's bosom? Then when I die she will not take me into her bosom to rest. You ask me to cut grass and make hay and sell it, and be rich like white men! But how dare I cut off my mother's hair? Will her cries never be heard again? Will we bequeath to her only tombstones with a sad tale to tell?

Felicitations

Awards and accolades in recognition of the saga of sacrifice stretching over fifty decades are naturally large in number.

NATIONAL AWARDS

1. Padmashri (1971): Returned as protest against building of giant dams in the country to the President of India in 1991.
2. Padma Vibhushan (1986)
3. Welfare of the Disabled (1986)

INTERNATIONAL AWARDS

1. Damien Dutton Award-USA, 1983 (Highest International Award for leprosy workers).

Nagpur Times

November, 17th 1983

Padmashri Baba Amte, well-known humanist and founder of Anandwan, has been awarded the prestigious International Damien Dutton Award for 1983 for his innovative work in the field of leprosy.... The award which is the highest recognition in the field of leprosy was instituted in the name of legendary Belgian Priest Fr. Damien and his American co-worker Dutton, in 1953.... Dr. Dharmendra, an octogenarian, internationally known Emeritus Scientist and Chairman for 1984 International Leprosy Congress, is the only other Indian recipient of this honour in 1970. It might be of interest to know that Baba Amta obtained initial training in leprosy under Dr. Dhramendra at the Tropical School for Medicine, Calcutta. Late American President John F. Kennedy was also honoured posthumously for introducing 'World Leprosy Day'.

Star Magazine, USA, March–April 1984: 'One of the highlights of my recent trip to India was the opportunity during the 12th International Leprosy Congress, to present the Damien Dutton Society 1983 Award to Murlidhar Devidas Amte, known affectionately as Baba Amte. He received this award in recognition of his life of outstanding service in the rehabilitation of Hansen's disease patients.' – Dr. Margaret Brand, National Hansen's Disease Centre, Carville, USA.

2. Ramon Magsaysay Award (1985)

The Times of India
Editorial

August 7, 1985

Once in a while a major international award is given to someone whose choice is so obvious and universally acceptable that it seems amazing that he was not chosen earlier. This is the case with Baba Amte, social worker extraordinary, who has just been awarded the Ramon Magsaysay Award, Asia's equivalent to the Nobel Prize. Baba Amte has become a legend in his lifetime. His use of indigenous and intermediate technologies to transform most barren of regions into agricultural Edens has been referred to time and again by both Indian and foreign agricultural and economic experts. Lady Barbara Ward, Third World economist and recipient of the Nehru Award (who donated the money she received to Amte) has long recommended Amte for the Nobel Prize.

Indian Express–Madras
Sunday, August 4, 1985

Mr. Amte, is the second person to be awarded Asia's version of the prestigious Nobel Prize this year. Baba Amte is a charismatic figure, who recently played an active role in movement against two dams on the Godavari and Indravati rivers. He has taken the stand that the construction of these dams will wipe out the Madia tribals.

The Hindu
Sunday, August 4, 1985
Manila, August 3, 1985

Social activist Murlidhar Devidas Amte will receive the Ramon Magsaysay Award for public service. Baba Amte, as he is popularly known, 'is recognized for his work-oriented revitalization of persons afflicted with leprosy and other handicapped outcasts,' the award foundation said in a statement. The Magsaysay Award, given yearly to Asians and non-Asians in five fields, is named after the Philippine president who died in 1957 in a plane crash while in office.

Magsaysay Award speech of Baba (excerpts):

I want to fly like a Madia tribal's arrow quivering with sun-intoxicated raptures to thank you for the honour done to me by conferring this highest Asian Award for public service. But as I am tied to my torture-stake of pain, I am requesting and deputing my son Dr. Vikas Amte to receive it on my behalf....

...I am really distressed by my disability. It is better to be healthy than to be famous. But God has given me supreme power to smile through the tears. Confidence and courage are my strongest shield and sharpest weapon...

...This award will lead me to deeper commitments. Now I summon my heart to my lips to thank you once again and request you to accept the tribute of a spontaneous tear offered by afflicted humanity of the disabled world.

3. U.N. Human Rights Award 1988, for outstanding contribution to humanity:

   Jan Marterson, Under Secretary General for Human Rights, wrote to Baba, 'I am pleased to inform you that you are the recipient of one of the Human Rights prizes.'

   'A formal ceremony for the award of the prizes will take place in the General Assembly Hall in New York at a commemorative session for the 40th anniversary of the Universal Declaration on 8th December 1988.... It is an honour for me to invite you to take part in this ceremony...'

India Abroad (International Weekly Newspaper), Friday, December 16, 1988, reported:

> Baba Amte, an activist who has worked for the rights of the handicapped in India, was given the Human Rights Award by the United Nations, last week.
>
> He was one of the six people to receive the award for their 'outstanding contribution to the promotion and protection of human rights.' C. R. Gharekhan, the Indian representative at the world organization, received the award on behalf of Baba Amte from Secretary General Perez de Cuellar.

4. G.D. Birla International Award, 1988, for outstanding contribution to humanity.

5. The Templeton Prize, 1990- U.K (U.S $ 6,84, 000, divided), world's largest cash prize and popularly known as Nobel Prize for Religion:

   'Baba Amte wins Templeton Award' – New York, March 7, 1990 (AP)

   Social worker Baba Amte and an Australian scientist were today named winners of the Templeton Prize for progress in religion. Biologist-geneticist, Charles L. Birch and Murlidhar Devidas Amte will share the 6,84,000 dollar prize, the largest made in any field.

The prize was founded in 1972 by financier John Templeton, a Presbyterian, who keeps the amount higher than the Nobel prizes in the belief that religion is more important.

'Work is my religion' Nagpur,– March 7th

'Work is my religion, for work builds, I believe', said Baba Amte before embarking upon his mission to the banks of the Narmada river to lead a national struggle against the monstrous dams. He was interpreting as to why he was chosen for the prestigious Templeton Award of 1990.

The Templeton Foundation has said in its official position on the criteria of choosing a person for the award, in effect, that the work of the nominee must result into a deeper spiritual awareness on the part of man, a better understanding of the meaning of life, a heightened quality of devotion and love...which will release new and creative energies into human society today.

Baba Amte is the third Indian to receive the Templeton Prize for Progress in Religion. Dr. S. Radhakrishnan, former President of India, when he was Professor of Eastern Religions at Oxford, had won the award. Mother Teressa is the other Indian to win the award for her work among the dying and destitute of the world.

Hinduism Today (International issue),
July 1990

Dr. Vikas Amte received the world's most valuable award on his father's behalf from Prince Philip at a ceremony at Buckingham Palace May 8th. Royalty, Rolls-Royce and most proper afternoon pinstripe suits were the order of the day. But reflecting the unpretentiousness of his father, Vikas was sporting the traditional Maharashtrian white kurta–pyjama outfit, which looked so simple that he was asked to show his invitation card by the ushers at the Guildhall reception. They did not realize he had in his hand a check for $279,000, his father's share of the famed Templeton Prize for Progress in Religion, nor that he was the main speaker at the event about to begin.

Cannon Edward Finch, who nominated Baba for the Templeton Prize, said in his introduction, 'Amte's leadership never issues from above and beyond the people, but always from within their amidst. Very Indian in his roots, Amte, through his work, is restoring and revitalizing the profound ideals of his country's faith....

During a 1987 visit to Anandwan, writer Gokul Gokhale of California asked Baba what kind of epitaph he'd like on his grave. Baba said, 'I would like a line on "crossed checks"– to mean a man who said responsibility is not transferable!'

The Templeton Prize 1990 acceptance speech as read out by Dr. Vikas Amte (excerpts):

> The award is a tribute to the spirit of thousands of people with whom I have worked – whose faith and determination have carried us through a path of compassion and creativity towards the deepest realms of spirituality.
>
> At Anandwan, the place where I have lived for the last 40 years, we have in our midst a memorial to an anonymous tree. As I lie down in my Fowler's bed, I listen to the whisperings from its grave: 'I have experienced the drowsiness of every autumn and the passions of every spring, hence I do not seek dust in shame and loneliness. Why do you?'
>
> The tree speaks to all who despair and sends them the message of renewal. When the tree sheds its leaves, the knowing celebrate the birth of living humans. When I consider the young, I cannot but think of them as new leaves, emerging from the nutrients of the leaf litter on the forest floor. They are the future.
>
> From Anandwan I bring to all of you the message of hope. A hope, that springs from a life-long journey in search of men. An odyssey rooted in one of the world's most ancient spiritual traditions. A tradition which like so many others seems enveloped today in the forces of darkness. And yet its

essential teachings every moment shatter the darkness and shine through radiant, like the rays of the Sun.

Today, the medium of the moment is violence everywhere. Man has become a transgressor. His arrogance, his belief in his power to control and order the universe, is crossing every reasonable limit. Technology, the supposed liberator, today stands as a potential agent of untrammelled destruction.

At such a moment we must seek a new way – a way which emerges from the roots of Mother Earth – which as it spreads embraces the plants, leaves, birds, animals, trees, valleys, mountains and rivers. A path, which ushers in greater kindness, tolerance and mutual respect towards all forms of life. A movement towards the rediscovery of the eternal, towards its recollection.'

6. International Giraffe Award – USA 1990

7. Global 500 – U.N Award, 1990

8. Right Livelihood Award – Sweden, 1992, for vision and work contributing to making life more whole, healing our planet and uplifting humanity. The Right Livelihood Awards are presented annually in the Swedish Parliament in Stockholm on the day before the Nobel Prize presentations. The awards are presented by the Right Livelihood Awards Foundation, a charity set up on the Isle of Man (British Isles) with representatives in England, Sweden and the United States. The idea and the original funding came from Jacob Von Uexkull, a Swedish–German writer and philatelic expert, who is director of the foundation and member of the European Parliament.

9. International Gandhi Peace Prize (1999)

Excerpts of the speech of the then P.M. Shri. Atal Bihari Vajpaye on the occasion of conferring the International Peace Prize upon Baba:

His personality cannot be measured in terms of Awards won by him. All his estates, all his earnings he spent for the

> good of the society. Not limiting his field of service, he devoted himself not only to the service of leprosy patients but also of the job of strengthening the nation...service not as charity or pity, not as some obligation on the persons to be served so that no inferiority complex will develop in the mind of the one who is being served. He has thus created an ideal, a goal for others to follow. Babasaheb is a poet at heart and is very sensitive. He realizes the sufferings of others and actively tries to remove them...
>
> Whatever he thinks is right, he sticks to it with firmness, but at the same time does not allow difference of opinion to come in the way of relationships. I would like to quote some lines from his own poems. He has said that hand should not be raised either for a fight or for begging. Nobody should spread his palm for alms but should stand on his own legs and live with self respect. By congratulating him I find myself honoured. Just now he was telling me about how old he is! I find it difficult to believe it that he is that old. Even at this age, he is working to knit, not split India.

Excerpts from the then President Shri. K.R. Narayanan's speech:

> Baba Amte is a living legend of our times and a shining example of the Gandhian spirit and approach to current and compelling social problems of the country. By crusading for human dignity and sustainable development he has sought to arouse the inner vitality of our society and invest it with sanity, peace and compassion.
>
> Baba Amte's life and activities have been animated by the constructive programme devised by Mahatma Gandhi for attainment of independence for India.... He is perhaps the first man in the post-independence India who has so passionately carried forward the Gandhian movement to see the glow of Swaraj on the face of the common man and woman our country. Baba Amte, like Mahatma Gandhi, remains a remarkably modern man. As a passionate and tireless social activist, he has been propagating his ideas

among the common people, specially among the youth of the country.

In our developmental efforts India and the world have to willy-nilly, come to terms with the ideas of Baba Amte. Baba Amte is a universal man united with suffering of mankind. Who else is there than this noble soul who is entitled to receive the Gandhi Peace prize?'

Excerpts from Baba's acceptance speech of the Gandhi Peace Prize:

> I have accepted this International Gandhi Peace Prize for the year 1999 on behalf of my family members, leprosy afflicted patients, the physically handicapped, the blind, the deaf-mute, the orphans, the homeless, the tribals, who all have remained unprotesting for an agonizingly long time. And also accept this on behalf of youth on whose breath the spine of the nation lives erect.
>
> Gandhiji whose whole life was sterilized with truth, love, compassion and non-violence and under whose invisible surveillance I am leading my life of loving, living and healing. I courted voluntary imprisonment for more than five decades with my depressed, oppressed, lonely leprosy patients and the socially deprived at Anandwan. You know people test you before they entrust you with your work. It is well known that a just place for a just man in an unjust society is either jail or death. Gandhiji aspired for both and courted both…
>
> I want to carry out His work till I lie down in the silent company of Mother Earth. Like spastic patients I pray: God please make my body my friend. It's not listening to my will. It's disobeying the command of my soul.

10. Dr. Ambedkar International Award-1999, for social change, by Government of India.

11. Paulos Mar Gregorios Award for Creative Compassion, by the Sophia Society of the Indian Orthodox Church.

Outlook

Views–counter views, observations–opinions, criticisms–praises? They all come aplenty in lives of people like Baba Amte. Amte belongs to a small league of men whose work, words and lives are, to the larger humanity, incomprehensible as well as awe-inspiring. These are the men who bequeath to posterity not only their names, but bodies of such work as are aspired for and emulated on the one hand and analysed and criticized on the other. These are the men who break the rules; these are the men who create their own standards; the men who defy the world; the men who create history. These are the men of steel. Little wonder then that these men are put under the microscope.

Tongues began wagging long, long ago when a teenaged Murlidhar Devidas Amte began defying standard norms of society. Eating, playing and interacting with the social outcasts, he was unwary of the wrath of even his own father. His own father turned his greatest critic. The two never saw eye-to-eye. Baba gently moved apart. 'It is not always correct to obey your parents, especially when they are wrong. If you do, you will never be able to do anything else in life,' the clarity of his assertion knocked me over. It must have been a pain wrought partition with his father, but in order for him to build new standards and renew rules, Baba snapped his filial bondage. And no one, save his mother, approved. He was alone in the midst of disapprovals and depreciations of his actions, by all and sundry. But he held on, confident of the fact that he was here to herald the dawn of a new era of thought. This confidence came from a well-done homework. He studied lives of men like

Marx and Ruskin, apostles like Christ and Buddha, and the ideals of his contemporaries like Gandhi, Vinoba and Tagore arrested his imagination. His mind was made up, his path was clear. And when finally the maggot-infested leper Tulsiram literally gave him the last push, since then he has never looked back.

People talked, posed problems, appreciated, joined him – whatever they did, the restlessness of his soul never had time to contemplate upon them. 'I have no time to even pray,' he has said, and it is not that he is a non-believer. He sought the remotest patch of earth and the most destitute and downtrodden, half a dozen men, to create a world with new standards, leaving this world to conjecture and comprehend, as it will. Anandwan –The Garden of Joy – the poem of a poet at heart, was begot with years of tears and toil. Yet even more than half a century later, many people look upon Anandwan with not so benevolent a gaze. This is partly because it is still seen more as a leper's colony, inspite of its expansion and ventures into other avenues and is thus stigmatized. One also wonders whether some of this is partly due to the projection of Baba as a figure associated with public fame. When one talks of Anandwan, one always thinks of Baba. So much has been said and written about him that some tend to view the man rather than his work as worthy of praise. 'There are some people,' Vikas speaks, evidently agitated, 'who even say that Baba has 'used' these leprosy patients to build Anandwan and still uses them as cheap labour. They don't see that he used them to build Anandwan for themselves! Not for him or his family. We also live here and work here, like them. We have no special benefits or richer lifestyles. We eat with them in the community kitchens.' But what do the residents, the healed and healing lepers and other physically handicapped at Anandwan, think? Do they feel exploited, used? I sought out and spoke with men, women and children – tilling the land, weaving, cooking, operating machinery, making and mending shoes, growing flowers, milking cows – for all of them Baba was only another name for God! 'But for him we would not even have been alive. When our own flesh and blood turned us out, Baba took us in with love and care. We would gladly give up our lives for him and you talk of exploitation.' All this was said with the same familiar enigmatic Anandwan special smile. The innocence and honesty of these smiles would not let even a slight shadow of doubt pass over the truth of their words of sheer worship for their loving Baba. 'Smiles are more infectious than disease at Anandwan,' the truth of Baba's words sunk in now after talking to the people who wore these smiles. And besides, if leprosy patients had been put to bed rather than work, how would Anandwan have been possible? Baba not only made, but makes them work, in order for them to realize their capacity for work and productivity, which in turn rekindles their lost dignity – wasn't this the idea on which he began Anandwan in the first place? If there was a compulsion to work, correspondingly there was a freedom to leave too. And it is not as if he set them upon hard labour while he sunned himself, he put himself too through such heavy manual labour that it literally broke his back and left his heart to beat on the mercy of pacemakers!

Going back into his childhood, Vikas comes back with some memories to make his point

> You know we were brought up like the children of the leprosy patients. We went to the same schools that they attended, ate the same food, had no friends other than them and even used their language. Often we would embarrass our parents when we went out as a family because both Prakash and me were loud and even abusive. Once when Sister Lila was staying at Anandwan, she convinced Baba that both of us brothers be sent to a good boarding school. All arrangements were made for us to attend the famous Doon School, at Dehradun. But when the moment came for us to go, Baba refused to send us. He said the whole purpose of his life and work would be defeated if his sons were to attend such a school while he sat at Anandwan and preached about equality and hard work. We had no special privileges as Baba's children. We still don't.

I had no further questions. As for Vikas's claim about the Amte family not having any special privileges, I found ample proof to ascertain it in the simple white cotton kurta–pyjama of Vikas, the even simpler and skimpier vest and long shorts of Prakash, their humble dwellings and still humbler menu.

This is not the end of critical attacks levelled against Baba. In fact it is just the beginning. For example, there are people who wonder that in spite of Baba's own example of dedicated service, his capacity for inspiring people and instilling in them self-esteem, it is surprising that the number of young people who have volunteered and stay on and work in his projects is rather small. The general pattern has been that of short-term commitment. Young people come with fervour, stay around for a little while and then go away. There are even some who have gone on to become his staunch critics. Mr. Jagdish Godbole, who was once an enthusiastic worker and had written several articles in praise of Baba's work, later began viewing it skeptically. He has described the entire experience as unusual, thrilling, realistic and at the same time disappointing. In course of time he began to dislike the way of functioning of the organization and found the atmosphere 'stifling' mainly because he felt that the Amte family made all the decisions. He has said that there was hardly any acceptance of opinions coming from other quarters. He has pointed out that Baba's social position of eminence and prestige prevented his work associates from expressing any disagreement or voice of dissent.

Dr. Kumar Saptarshi and his wife, well-known activists, were eager to work in Somnath. Before making his final decision, Dr. Saptarshi had approached Baba for certain clarifications. What would be his role in the project? What would be the extent of his freedom in decision-making, independent of Baba? What was the blueprint for further developments? From where would the funds come? Baba, he writes, seems to have been annoyed by these questions, for which he did not give any answers. Baba responded with a counter question, 'Did the disciples of Jesus Christ ask for a blueprint when they followed him?' This stance was unacceptable to Dr. Saptarshi with the unavoidable result that he gave up his plan of working in Somnath. Associates like Mr. Datye think it is unfair to expect blueprints from Baba. The projects that he has hitherto developed were based on well-thought-out plans, even though they were not laid out on precisely defined blueprints.

Some people, specially youngsters, on a superficial wave of enthusiasm and idealism, decide to work at Anandwan or in other centres, but their potential for sustained work in such settings is rather limited, with the outcome that frustration sets in easily. Some of them come with personal frustrations, viewing the work as offering an avenue to curb these. The monotony of routine activities, the simple lifestyle, the rural environment without much facilities, conveniences and pleasures of urban living, and the isolation from towns and cities add to their frustration. It is obvious that the incentive for involvement in such projects is neither monetary considerations nor a comfortable life. The only incentive is the satisfaction that can be derived from doing work in a programme of service geared to the goal of development of the socially handicapped people. Not many are willing to live and work for such an incentive alone. There are also certain limitations while living as part of a community. Alcohol is prohibited, and strict schedules are to be followed if one wants to avail oneself of the services of the community kitchen. It is likely that some of the volunteers feel their freedom somewhat thwarted by these restrictions, even though they are attracted to the projects. Inspiration from others and ideals shining at a distance cannot compensate for the lack of a strong inner conviction which generates and is generated within an individual. A few young people who were drawn towards the development projects were social activists who were eager to take such radical steps as were not in Baba's scheme of things, and hence they were disillusioned and in the end left him.

While there have been several who have departed, there are a few others who are less enthusiastic about their support, though they remain with him in public. They denounce him as an autocrat. There have been hushed complaints against him of being dominating and authoritarian in his approach. He has been criticized for not even listening to, let alone using suggestions of others associated with his projects. One of his critics has ascribed this to his 'Zamindari' (landlord) background, 'Baba, like a true "Zamindar", is habituated to wielding power over others.' How unfortunate as well as ironic that the man who shed caste distinctions long ago, who gave up his Brahminical practices and rituals, who relinquished the rights to his ancestral property and finally who has created a caste-free and secular Anandwan, is still being criticized by some as being a Brahmin and 'Zamindar'. The intellectually oriented and ideologically based have found it most difficult to live with Baba. Their bent of mind necessitates a thorough analysis and ongoing assessment of the rationale for the work, the strategies and the style of leadership to be adopted for bringing about the change. But Baba by nature has had no patience for debate and questioning. He believes in the power of work to convince you and tide over uncertainty and hesitation. The notion of collective leadership is also not in tune with Baba's interest in action, and this may be the reason why his critics have often described him as autocratic. But Baba has said in his defence that from the time he started his leprosy work, his experience has been that most of the suggestions that came from others were negativistic; there was mostly disapproval, discouragement and words of undue caution. Consequently he began to rely more and more on his own intuition and planning. However, the time has come for a change in approach. What Baba has achieved needs to be maintained, consolidated and further developed by others. As he himself has said, that he does not need followers but successors. The successors need to be equipped in skills to carry on the work. A sense of participation through exchange of ideas and opinions is the best soil in which skills can develop. And Vikas humbly even accepts this. He gives a convincing reason for Baba's seemingly authoritarian attitude, 'You see Baba belonged to and began his work in an entirely different era from today. The common people then had rigid notions of caste and class, and besides they were poor and illiterate. When Baba showed them a different world that would have a place for them in it and one which they were capable of building themselves, at first they barely understood him. But when Anandwan became a fully functional reality, their gratitude to *the Man* was shown by nothing less than worship. These people barely had any ideas and suggestions to give Baba. As a result Baba had to voice his anger and frustrations in order to make them see the point, and they then followed him blindly. This made him appear autocratic in the eyes of the outsiders. Even to many of the educated people of those days, Baba's ideas were bizarre and in turn their suggestions to him could not apply to the scheme of his ideas and hence the criticism.' But Vikas fully understands that the times are entirely different now. The residents at Anandwan are educated and aware. They have views and opinions, which cannot be quashed. It is difficult for Baba to understand these times totally, and it would be unfair on him if anyone were to expect that from him at this age now. 'But you see,' continues Vikas, 'we've already started making changes and accommodations here. We don't put any restrictions on living anymore. They are allowed to cook and eat non-vegetarian food in their rooms, if they wish and even consume alcohol if they wish! They are allowed to study and pursue a career outside the precincts of the community if they want. I personally take time out every day to listen to their suggestions, complaints, requests and grievances. There are many times when Baba does not approve of the changes that we make here, he still gets angry and agitated. It's a generation gap, which is nothing new, only natural. But some people read too much into it.'

Baba is also known to have had occasional bouts of temper outbursts, which according to some of his friends are often found in a man who is in a hurry to get things done. His critics have pointed out that his temper makes him unapproachable in situations in which a thrashing out of different views is necessary. He has even been accused of raising his hand, but those who have been on the receiving end of his temper have seen and experienced the love and care behind this harsh action. Aggressiveness is in the nature of most of the achievers who have made history. It is this aggressive energy, which gets channelled into great works. Perhaps had it not been for this aggressive vitality, Baba would not have been able to achieve what he has. It was his fighting spirit, which probably helped him survive the ordeals he has had to encounter. He strove physically to tame an unfriendly terrain and mentally, to break down the prejudices and rigidities of society. Such a formidable task perhaps necessitated an aggressive approach. Even at 90 years, the fierceness and the vitality is evident in his eyes. He looks one so straight in the eye that perforce the other's gaze begins to waver in the face of so great an intensity, even at the age of 90! It would not be unbelievable to anyone who has met him, even if recently, that he must have owned an extremely aggressive personality.

Communication is a two-way process involving speaking and listening. A good communicator is one who not only talks relevantly, but also listens with equal ardour to the other person's views. Some people, both among Baba's friends and adversaries, are of the opinion that he is not an effective communicator. Their criticism is that he does not listen to what others have to say. His words and ideas surge forth so torrentially that the other person finds it difficult to get in even a word in edgeways. A friend of Baba's has observed that a conversation with him soon turns into a monologue. In a conversation of two people of disparate social status, the less prominent of the two needs encouragement from the other to be able to express feelings, opinions or ideas, so that an element of mutuality or reciprocity may be brought about. This mutuality is sadly missing in the relationships of many great personalities, including that of Mahatma Gandhi. Apparently, this is precisely what happened in Baba's case too. Baba is unable to take his listener along with him into his stream of thinking. He skips from topic to topic without providing links, with the result that the taxing task of linking up the material, falls on the listener. But with his patients Baba is most patient!

It is well over three decades since the birth of the Lok Biradari Prakalp (LBP) or People's Brotherhood Project at Hemalkasa. It has developed firm roots and is better accepted by the tribals at Hemalkasa than the Anandwan project is by the locals at Warora. The simple reason for this is that the LBP is situated far away in a solitary wilderness and is thus shielded from the constant scrutiny of the public and media gaze that Anandwan is constantly exposed to. The Hemalkasa tribals and their beneficiaries are therefore enjoying a happy co-existence without the interference of third parties that can often become the cause of doubt and friction between two groups.

During my tour of the project with Prakash, as we stand under the embrace of the 'benevolent mango tree', under which Baba had camped with his family many years ago, I can feel the complete calm of the place. I try to enter the minds of the young Amte siblings, lying on the bare earth, as their father narrated to them the tales of woes of the tribals, trying in the process to awaken their young consciences to see and feel the abject plight of the Madias. These stories must have so gripped the young mind of Prakash, making him give up not only his studies, but also a cosy comfortable urban life. Breaking my reverie, Prakash points to a dilapidated structure, further on from where we are standing. It is an unfinished Church, says Prakash. Christian missionaries had tried to impregnate the tribal area with their presence, with a view to doing social work there. But the hostilities of both the tribals as well as the Naxalites made a failure of their intentions and endeavours. 'However, we managed to stay on, despite all the challenges,' added Prakash, who is frugal with words. This does not spare the LBP from being attacked by the criticisms of those that have reservations about the utility and success of the project. These people believe that the LBP is only a new form of the Christian mission that enters a backward area, starts schools and health centres and provides guidance – technical and spiritual. It does not go beyond this. There is hardly any attempt at building awareness among the tribals, about their exploitation nor of organizing them. There is blind experimentation and a lack of vision at times. These allegations are serious and disturbing.

Then what, one doubtfully may ask, was Baba's vision about Hemalkasa? To some it was an impulse, a challenge and an adventure, on which he launched the project sans a vision. To others, it was a dream of putting back the smile on the faces of the Madia tribals, that he had seen when he visited it as a fourteen-year-old. To still others, a bit of both. To me, a most courageous effort that has borne healthy fruit. What if the work at LBP is on the lines of Christian missionaries, what if a lot has been done but a lot more needs to be done, what if. But the skeptics need to answer this one first – are there any others who dared and succeeded in reaching out to the woebegone tribals? Baba in his own words has said that he wanted to put back the smile on the faces and the trust in the hearts of the exploited tribals. He began with this humble vision. Baba's vision realized by Prakash in spite of the shortcomings that the skeptics see in it, was tough to even have been envisioned, let alone attempted.

Prakash is in complete charge of the LBP today, with his wife Manda, son Dr. Digant, sister Renuka and brother-in-law Vilas, assisting him zealously. Prakash presents an antithesis to Baba's personality in some aspects and resembles him closely in some others. Like Baba, he is adventurous and has few qualms about taking risks; unlike Baba he is reserved and speaks little. He jokes about the critics, dismissing their remarks with nothing more than a shrug. Any amount of probing and prodding for eliciting any kind of reaction from him regarding the criticisms helps but little, 'I will do what my conscience tells me. To hell with what people say,' is all one gets. Prakash even more than Baba has reservations about receiving aid from others, 'If aid is too conditional, I will refuse it.' He is the least flustered about the criticisms levelled against the Amte clan and their work. He is even amused by the fact that many of their worst critics have not even visited the projects. A single visit to the LBP project puts to rest all apprehensions. An amalgamation of faith, love and respect oozes unabashedly from the faces of the tribals, while they chatter away with Prakash in their alien language, which the latter has mastered. These people have included Prakash, Baba and Tai in all aspects of their lives. Not only do they benefit from the LBP by availing the facilities of the hospital, school and modern agricultural techniques, but come to the Amte threshold to take the advice of its inmates on all issues – legal as well as personal – that bear upon their lives. None need any more proof of the genuineness of the efforts of Baba in his vision and its realization of the LBP project after a single visit to Hemalkasa.

Baba and his work have evoked different reactions from different people. He has been compared with the greats like Mahatma Gandhi, Vinoba Bhave, Veer Savarkar, Maharishi Karve and many such others. Many view him as a man of meritorious achievements and highly commendable qualities. Some can see his achievements as worthy of the highest praise but different from other great men. At the same time there are some who attack him with criticisms, uncomplimentary and derogatory remarks and even go so far as to cast aspersions on his motives. The conclusion – such an abundant repository of different viewpoints about one man, his life, his work, his words – is the surest sign of his greatness. He will be remembered in history as setting off on a journey that skeptics have described as unlikely to reach its eventual destination, but one that on the way will provide succour to all those that thirst for it at any time in their journeys.

At Anandwan there is one unpretentious, quiet little spot – the graveyard! This is perhaps the most beautiful and soulful tract of land that there can be. It is also the most unconventional kind of graveyard, bereft of any exquisitely chiselled marble headstones scripted with beautifully worded inscriptions. No grand granite statues that attempt to freeze men's personalities into strange stony expressions. No mounds of earth strewn with flowers to mark graves, no cobbled pathways leading to them, no incense sticks, no candles, nothing, save a wood of more than five thousand trees. Beneath the canopy of this wood have sprung a variety of wild flowers to form a carpet underneath which lie the bodies of those that lived, loved and died at Anadwan. Here lie over a hundred men, whose bodies have melted into the crust of the earth, providing nourishment to the trees that are planted over them. 'This kind of burial is Baba's way of showing gratitude to nature. In this way our dead bodies will be able to repay some of the heavy debt of nature's bounty that we have incurred in our lifetimes as we partook of its many splendours. Also it acknowledges that people belong to the land rather than the land belonging to the people,' said Vikas as I stood in complete awe. I came back to this place at dusk, the next evening. Just sat under a tree and soaked in the solitude and serenity because there are no ghosts which visit this wonderland, which is yet a graveyard! Baba wished to be laid to eternal rest in this grove until he decided to move to Kasarvad and shroud himself in the waters of the Narmada river in protest against the building of large dams. But since his return from Kasarvad two years ago, perhaps Baba's wish still stands. Perhaps this little graveyard will be the privileged one to hold in its embrace the enigma that was Murlidhar Devidas Amte, in an everlasting embrace, when the time comes. But before that time comes, it would be fitting to adorn the legend that is Amte, with the brightest jewel of the nation – the Bharat Ratna, by way of gratitude for his unrelenting six decades of selfless service.

Credits

1. *Baba Amte: The Man and His Mission* (Biography), by S.M. Shirodkar and Dr. B.G. Bapat.
2. Mr. Manoj Saranathan for allowing the use of material from the website *narmada.org*
3. Anna Weston, the Permission Administrator, for allowing the use of material from the *New Internationalist Online Magazine,* U.K.
4. Rajni Bakshi, for permitting the quotation of an excerpt from her book, *Bapu Kuti: Journeys in the Rediscovery of Gandhi.*
5. Dr. Vikas Amte for allowing the use of the intensely researched 'Documentation of Baba Amte's Work' by Tata Institute of Social Sciences (1988) and providing news clippings from various years as well as speeches of Baba and others during award giving ceremonies.

Baba Amte in 1936 as a young lawyer who took a fancy to pinstriped suits, fast cars, drinking beer and smoking

PICTURE GALLERY

Sadhna Tai at work at the *Shramashram* Project, which had to be abandoned later.

Water for the barren land

Young Vikas contributed his mite by keeping the home fires burning.

Turning Anandwan from wasteland to wonderland

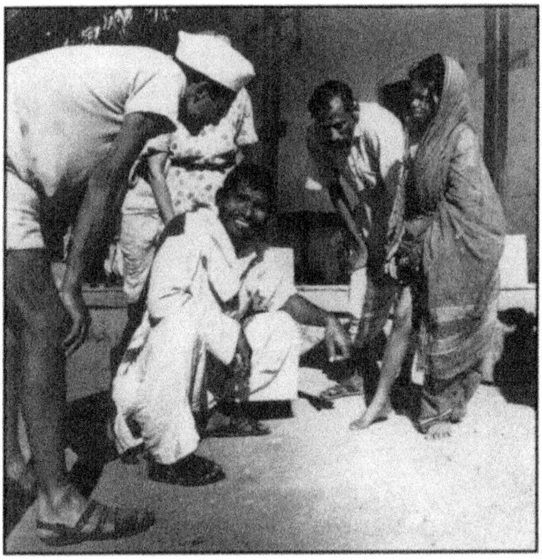

Baba tending to leprosy patients during early days at Anandwan

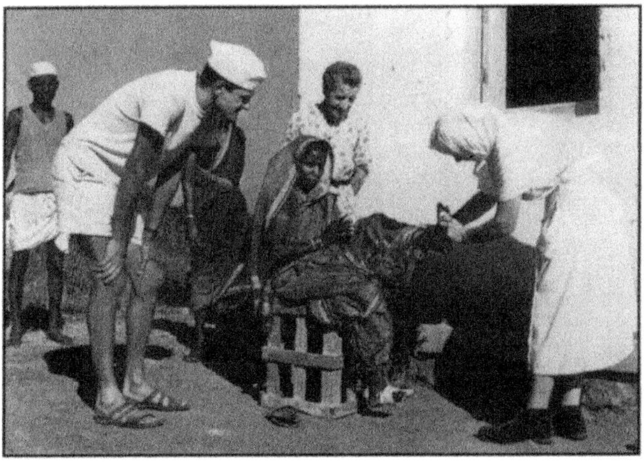

Mother Gavrilia, affectionately known to the Anandwan family as Sister Leela, tending to a patient

Anandwan inmates.

Handloom weaving unit

Woodwork unit

Welding unit

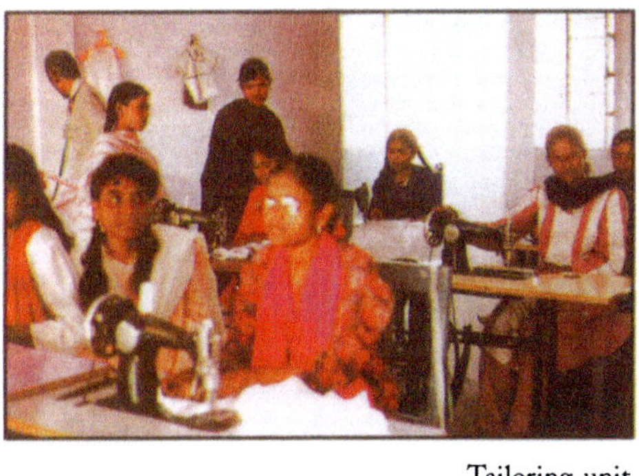

Tailoring unit

The Community Kitchens of Anandwan

The Anandwan Dairy Farm

A Community marriage ceremony at Anandwan.

Outside Ashokwan Project, which was established in 1956

PICTURE GALLERY

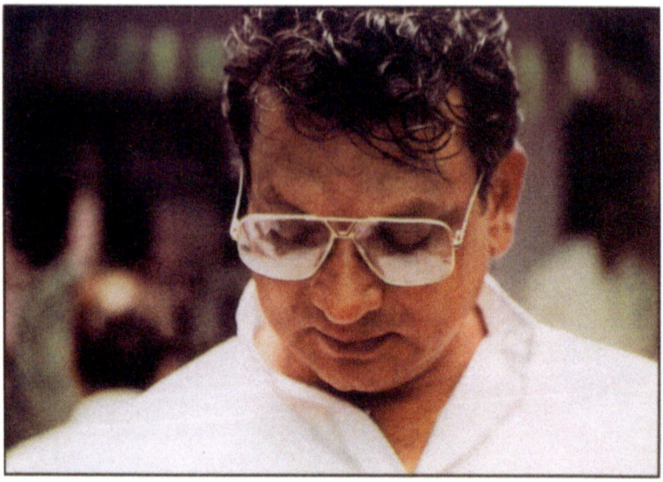

Vikas taking charge of Anandwan

Anandwan–The Garden of Joy.

At Anandwan

Marianne Lusch, Baba Amte's adopted German daughter, has been a friend of Anandwan since 1973.

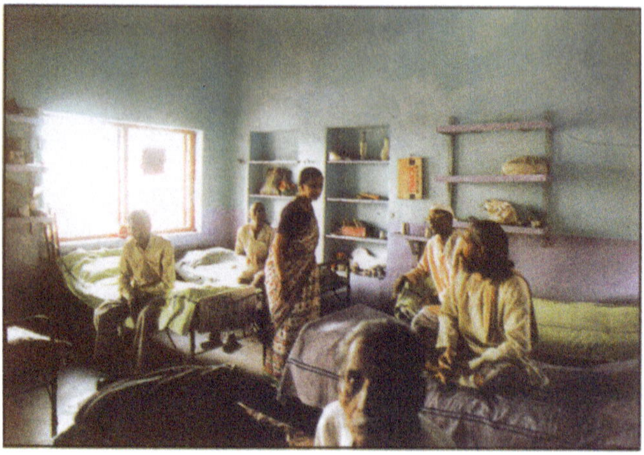

Sadhna Tai with the Patients.

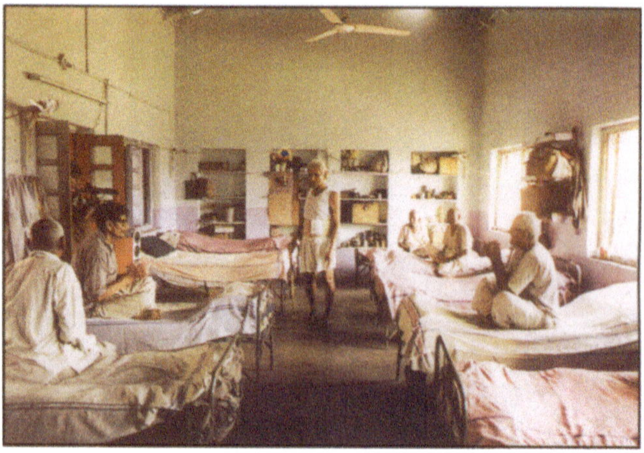

Baba at the Anandwan Hospital.

Sadhna Tai crossing the river on foot
to reach camp Hemalkasa

Prakash at the Animal Orphanage.

Amte family at the first hut at Hemalkasa. Sitting L to R – Renuka (Baba's adopted daughter) and Prakash. Standing L to R – Tai, Baba and Vikas.

Dr. Mandakini at work with her son Dr. Digant

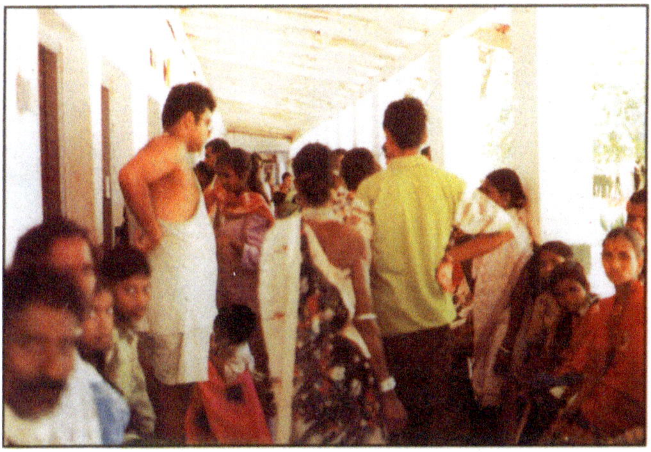

Hundreds of patients come daily to the hospital traversing long and difficult terrain on foot.

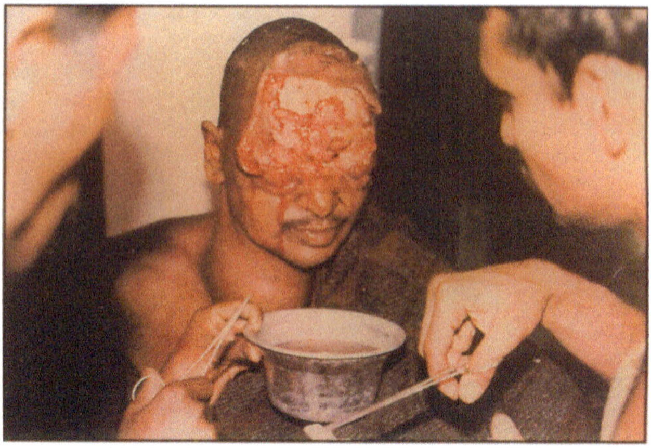

The victim of a bear bite has lost his sight and had his scalp split open.

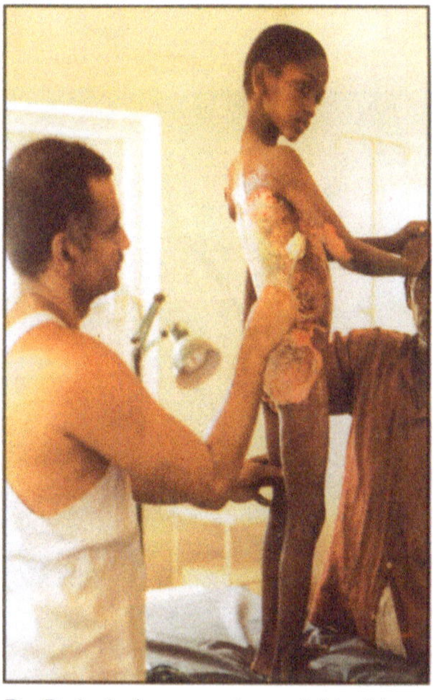

Dr. Prakash Amte treating a child with severe burns

Alfred Knans of Service Civil International

The Service Civil International (SCI) team with Baba and Tai

One of the last photographs of Baba in sitting posture. Also in the picture, Baba's lifelong associate and renowned Gandhian Annasaheb Sahasrabuddhe.

With Gyanpeeth Award winner V.V. Shirwadkar (Shakespeare of Maharashtra), who described Baba as a Maha Manav (great human being)

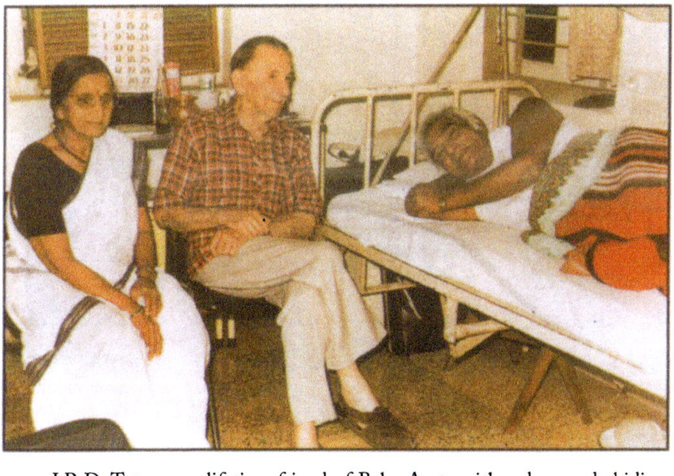

J.R.D. Tata was a lifetime friend of Baba Amte with a deep and abiding commitment to Baba's life mission.

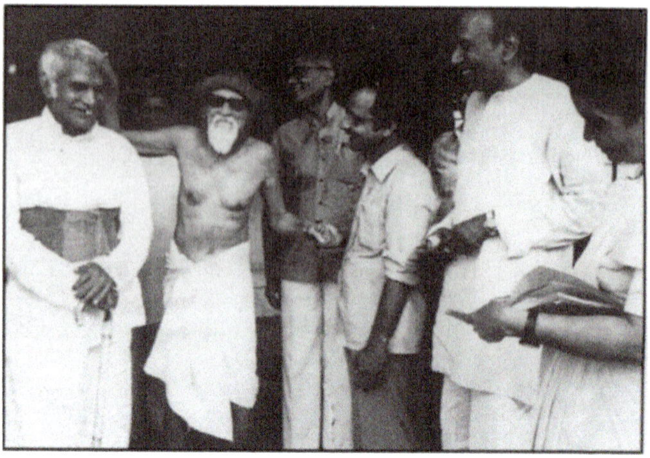

With his mentor Vinoba Bhave. Baba has said of him, 'On his shoulders I stood to get a glimpse of the new horizons that beckoned me.'

The legendary P. L. Deshpande, grand old man of Marathi theatre, was a close and committed friend of Baba Amte.

His Holiness the Dalai Lama and Baba

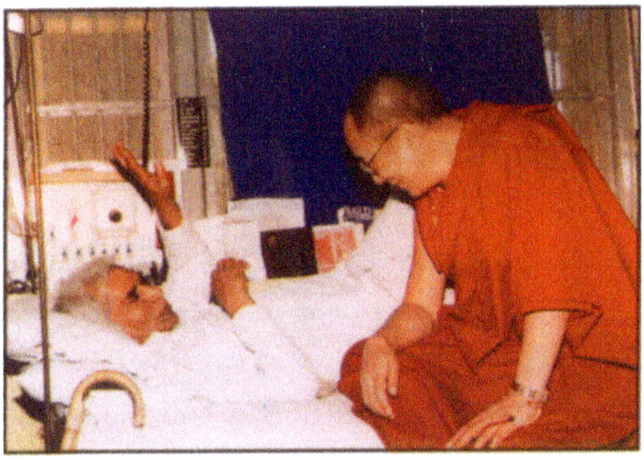

Two soulmates in communion.

On the banks of river Narmada

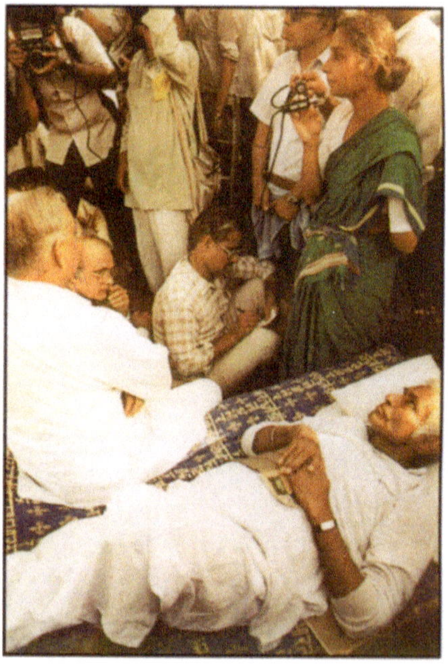

Outside his hut on the banks of the Narmada. Also in the picture, NBA activist Medha Patkar addressing a press conference.

Baba Amte and Sadhna Tai addressing the youth camp held in the summer of 2000

Receiving the Gandhi Peace Prize for 1999 from the then
Prime Minister Shri A.B. Vajpayee and President Shri K.R. Narayanan.